worth the squirm

worth the squirm

How Our Business Helps Us Heal

Sarah Stokes

BIRCH & blue skies BOOKS

Worth the Squirm
Copyright © 2025 by Sarah Stokes
ISBN 979-8-218-60269-7
Published by Birch & Blue Skies Books

All rights reserved.

This book is non-fiction and primarily based on actual events. The stories reflect the author's present recollections of experiences over time, and may not match the recollections of other persons who lived these same events. Some names and characteristics have been altered or excluded to protect the privacy of the persons involved, some events may have been compressed, and some dialogue has been recreated.

The author has made every attempt to provide information that is accurate and complete, but this book is not intended as a substitute for professional medical advice. This book is not meant to be used, nor should it be used, to diagnose or treat any medical or psychological condition. Readers are advised to consult their own medical advisors whose responsibility it is to determine the condition of, and best treatment for, the reader.

Any quotations that do not have citations are from the author's personal experience.

Editing, cover design, flower illustration, and formatting by Mission and Media – missionandmedia.com

Contents

Setting Intentions

A Note from Sarah   *3*

Dedication   *5*

Your Juicy Good Life   *7*

Sent to Help You Heal

Choose Your Perspective   *11*

How I Use Words   *15*

We Thought Wrong   *21*

The Biggest Catalyst   *23*

I Didn't See It for Years   *27*

You Don't Have to Force It   *31*

Created for Purpose

Your Business Chose You   *35*
Your Why   *41*
Your Business Name   *47*
Your Mission, Vision, and Values   *55*
The Results We Want   *63*

Designed for Connection

It Kicks Up All of Our Stuff   *71*
Numb It or Heal It   *73*
Ninety Seconds or Ninety Years   *77*
Actors in Our Play   *85*
Our Customers and Clients   *89*
Our Team Members   *99*
Our Relationships   *107*

Braving Your Wounds

Naming the Wounds   *123*
They Change Outfits   *127*
Generational Trauma   *133*

People-Pleasing   *135*
Visibility   *143*
Limiting Beliefs   *153*
Workaholism   *159*
Money   *167*
Purchases   *179*
Receiving   *185*
Right on Time   *191*
We're Never Done   *195*

Befriending the Squirm

Becoming Ourselves   *201*
Worth the Payoffs   *207*
Efficiency   *209*
Getting Paid and Loving It   *213*
Liquid Gold Energy   *217*
Deeper Connections   *219*
The People We Meet   *223*
Building Trust   *225*
Making Room for Joy   *227*

Working Through the Squirm

Ten Steps of the Squirm *233*

Endnotes *239*
Recommended Follows *241*
This Is Not Goodbye *243*
Let's Stay Connected *245*
Meet the Author *247*

Setting Intentions

A Note from Sarah

It's worth the squirm. The squirm that comes with growing your business, my friend.

It is worth it.

Joy is worth it.

Ease is worth it.

Healing is worth it.

Welcome to the book that's written so you have a new way to align with your business, so you get that Juicy Good Life you want.

May it spark insight.

May it ripple infinite awareness.

May it reduce suffering.

May it amplify joy.

I love you,

Sarah Stokes

Business Joy Coach
Founder of The Juicy Good Life
Your "Goalmate" and Vision Holder

Dedication

A book saved my life. Not in the call-911-kind-of-way, but in the save-yourself, choose-freedom-and-joy kind of way. So, in honor of every author who has written a book, even though it felt scary, I will get out of my own way and write this one.

Dedicated to all the souls who bring more love to the world.

Dedicated to my incredible clients who do this work with me every day. I am forever grateful to get to watch you uplift the world.

Dedicated to my daughter, Kaydie, my son, Kanyon, and my husband, Chris. Thank you for giving me a reason to be a better me.

Dedicated to the memory of my brother, Tanner, whose untimely death helped me start to actually live.

Dedicated to my soul sister, Rachelle Guse, whose steadfast love has gotten me through the hardest times in my business and life. She's helped me grow, learn, heal, and seize the day.

Dedicated to all the wise women who helped me along my spiritual awakening and business path. To Dr. Jodi Ritsch, Dr. Aveen Banich, Katie Rubin, Laura Clark, and Serena Hicks, you have helped me heal my life for years. You've guided me through so many squirms.

Dedicated to Wendy Sloneker, Angela Nelson, Krystal Rappley, and Julie Olberding for cheering me on as I squirmed and procrastinated writing this book.

Dedicated to every human this book helps.

May the discoveries you'll make inside these pages reduce your suffering and amplify your joy.

Your Juicy Good Life

Setting intentions has been one of the most impactful business tools I've leveraged. I want to set powerful intentions as I write this book for you. I want this book to add Love with a capital L to your world.

By the end of this book, I hope you have insight that makes room for more gentleness in your days and joy in your business and life.

May you find ways to celebrate how incredible you and your business are as partners. May you begin to find evidence of its healing powers in your life. Signs of how it has already helped you become more you. That your business can become that wonderful dream you had.

May it flow alongside you and be a conduit for your Juicy Good Life.

Sent to Help You Heal

Choose Your Perspective

You get to choose how you want to use this book. Each of us brings our unique perspective to the books we read. You bring layers of your life to this book. Your lens.

Your lens brings into focus all the elements that make up your unique experience: strengths, dreams, generational trauma, maybe a "neuromagical" (neurodivergent) layer, your values, your roles, your achievements, and your human design. They all crisscross to make you who you are.

Honor all of the elements of you as you let this book help you uncover exactly what you need. How you choose your next steps will make all the difference as you embrace the squirm.

It can be a weapon or a tool. My invitation to you is that you choose to use it as a powerful tool in your toolbox. As we know, a hammer can help you build a house, but it could do some major damage if it is used as a weapon instead.

Let this book be a tool. A tool that brings incredible insight.

Now, I invite you to choose your perspective. How do you want to think about your business? See what resonates below, trust it, and go with it.

....

How do you want to think about your business?

....

When you think about the support you want by your side as you grow your business, which of these sound good to have?
- A best friend who is always there
- A powerful healer who transforms you
- A soul guide who directs you
- Or a new version of your own

It matters that you choose your perspective because for this to resonate, it needs to speak to your heart. If we think of our business as a loving energy in our life, it can remove so much resistance.

Together, you and your business can be a force of nature. Take a few moments to write out your perspective.

I choose to view my business as:

Great job! Now take that vision with you throughout the book. To keep viewing it as a tool, we can't be sitting in a you-versus-me mode with your business.

Let it be a partnership.

How I Use Words

What do I mean by the word *squirm*? Let's review some important notes before we get too far into the book.

After years of helping business owners like you, I noticed that some common words like *discomfort*, *hurdle*, *challenge*, and *problem* didn't quite describe the transformational process of a businesswoman amid deep change or pattern shifting.

Squirm seemed to land with my clients in a helpful way. You can feel it when you say it. When we deal with nervous systems, trauma responses, and a desire to grow, we squirm, but we don't die from it. It's going to feel like a (excuse my highly technical description here) "Ugh, heck no, don't wanna, show up shaking, kind of want to run or barf, but I know on the other side is what I want—so, fine, I'll love myself through this" vibe.

Your squirm will be different from my squirm.

My squirm comes with some resistance, tears, a few voice memos (or twenty) to my bestie, journaling, and then doing the dang thing and realizing once again it wasn't that awful.

As you read this book, you may meet your squirm in a new way. That is amazing. Yes, please. Get to know your squirm. She's here to help.

> **Your business can partner with you if you think about it as a loving energy.**

Yeah, I might personify a lot of words in this book too. *Money*, *your business*, and *joy* will be personified in a few different ways. Your business can partner with you if you think about it as a loving energy too (back to how you want to view it from earlier pages).

I will use the words *healing*, *healer*, *medicine*, and such as ways to describe evolution, change, and transformation.

Please know I'm speaking in energetic and awareness terms, not literal medical terms.

I use *universe*, *the divine*, and *God* interchangeably. What I mean by it is an unseen energy bigger than us. I understand this word usage is personal and means something unique to you. Please choose your resonant word and substitute it for whatever word I use if they differ.

I'll talk about your *soul*. I am referring to the highest expression of you.

I will use the word *conditioning*. In this book, it will mean the repeated messages we've been taught, seen in marketing over the years, and have absorbed from our childhood and adulthood.

You'll see the word *deconditioning*. This is meant to describe the unlearning we choose to do to uncover what we truly want from our life and business.

I'm known as the "Should Free" coach. I named an entire business program after it. In my work, I use the term *shoulds* to describe the things we think we have to do but aren't actually in alignment for us. Shoulds are different than commitments.

Commitments may feel like shoulds, but they are decisions we make that we want to follow through on because they are important to us. Feeding our kids and fur babies: commitment. Do we always love it? No. Is it important enough to follow through? Yes. A should is something you'll notice you don't want to follow through on—because it was never meant to be a yes from you in the first place.

Shoulds are different than commitments.

I'll talk about *wounds*. Not the kind you get stitches to fix. These are the unseen old hurts that manifest in different reactions and activations and have created protective parts and patterns for us. Wounds can be anything from a hurtful sentence someone said once all the way to "big T" trauma. Our wounds are unique to us, and healing them will be unique to you too. I am here to help you see how your business can bring them up to the light to be reviewed, not to pretend that's the only thing your wounds need. Please get the well-rounded support you need. Therapy, healing modalities, faith, etc. It's all valid, and please get your needs met. Healing is an ongoing and evolving process that is unique to each of us.

I want to honor that trauma rides shotgun in our businesses. So, when I use the word *triggered* (a stimulus that causes a painful memory to resurface), I am not taking it lightly or trying to use casual pop culture terms. Triggers are very real for us in business, and I haven't met a human who has zero trauma to heal from in adulthood.

> For the purpose of being a more loving and compassionate friend to yourself, let your healing matter.

That trauma varies, and depending on our perspectives, your brain may be judging the word right now. But for the purpose of being a more loving and compassionate friend to yourself, let your healing matter. Let your triggers simply be true for you. Don't put yourself in a comparison trap with someone who has it worse. These are more ways we dishonor ourselves.

Yes, there is incomprehensible trauma on this planet. I pray that has not been your situation, but many of the women I help have been through hell. I am not here to play games about who has it worse, and if you're drawn to my work, I know you try to care for everyone else first. This book is for you to be there for *you* and *your* story.

It matters that your trauma gets to be witnessed. Please seek professional assistance for your trauma healing. If this book can help you choose more support for your healing, that is a blessing.

I also use the word *joy*. I understand this is a loaded word sometimes. Cultural conditioning says joy is a certain holiday-card-worthy, Pinterest-inspired kind of moment or vacation or achievement.

I invite you to see this word in a new way with me.

Joy is what you decide it is for you. Whatever lights that spark of "Yay!" in your body. The experience that brings a well of tears up to your eyes from the middle of your swelling heart.

Joy is a shape-shifting birthright. It won't look the same today as it does tomorrow, but I want you on the lookout for it. It wants to be a fixture in your life.

You, me, us, we—I'm going to use it all and maybe in the same sentence. It might make a purist's eyes twitch. I get it. I'm a trained journalist, and I don't follow rigid rules anymore. Why? Because I have learned over years of connecting with the women I'm best here to serve, my writing needs to come from the heart. I found myself overthinking this many times, so I gave myself the gift of just putting a disclaimer up front. Feels better already!

I have an amazing editor, Michelle Rayburn. She is solid gold fantastic. She is going to do her best to make this book clean and easy to read, and if you notice inconsistencies, it's not her fault; it's me being free to write from the heart, following intuition, not from "shoulds" (which is my whole brand).

And finally, while I am a business coach, entrepreneur, and lady who wants to make the world better, I am not a psychologist or doctor. My intention is to help you build awareness and curiosity. My request of you is to tune in to this book with your soul and then seek support for anything it might kick up for you that needs professional attention.

We will squirm a bit, but I anticipate a lot of newfound curiosity and relief when you unlock what's meant for you to find in these pages.

Thanks for being here.
Thanks for doing what you do.
Squirming with you.
Here we go.

We Thought Wrong

Growing a business is one of the most courageous things we'll ever do. Why? Because it will literally kick up everything that wants healing.

Your money stuff?

Kicked up daily.

Your relationships and support system?

Oh, wowie, will you see where there are gaps.

Your over-giving? That will need attention.

Your perfectionistic tendencies?

They'll need a lot of deconditioning.

Your trauma responses?

They want to drive the bus until they get the loving connection they truly need.

The big myth out there in "start a business, grow a business" land is that growth is purely tactical.

A skill set outside of you to be mastered.

> **Growing a business is one of the most courageous things we'll ever do.**

What I have learned in more than a decade of helping entrepreneurs and personally growing multiple companies to multiple millions . . .

is that what actually had to grow . . .

. . . was me.

The Biggest Catalyst

Your business can be the biggest healing catalyst of your life. Nothing gets us showing up for growth like owning a business. If you feed your family with your business like I do, oh baby, are you going to want to and need to show up for all the things that make you squirm.

If we see our business as an ally that truly wants the best for us, it will likely be the same amount of squirm but a lot less suffering.

You will still be uncomfy when you do new things.

You will still bump up against old patterns.

You will still have days when you wonder if it's worth it.

You'll also have days where you want to squeeze and kiss your sweet business like a fluffy bunny because it absolutely delights you.

If you've been seeing your business as an oppressive cage, you will have the same amount of squirm but a lot *more* suffering.

You will see things as outside your control.

You will feel like challenges happen to you, not for you.

You will see threats everywhere.

You'll feel dread and avoidance when it comes time to show up.

You'll choose Band-Aid fixes and formulas and wonder why nothing is working.

Let's be a kinder partner to our business, and let our business love us back.

Let's open a bit, relax our shoulders a little, be a kinder partner to our business, and let our business love us back. I keep getting the image of a rose relaxing its petals, opening to more sunshine and oxygen. Can you imagine that for a moment? Find a rose in your favorite color in your mind's eye and just imagine it unfurling, going from a tight bud to an expansive, huge, jaw-droppingly beautiful bloom that takes your breath away.

What could get better in your life and business if you relaxed into more trust with the messages and lessons the business brings instead of taking them head-on like a ram trying to plow through struggles?

How can you already see your business as your ally? What has it done for you today that you haven't given it any gratitude for?

Today, my business allowed me to pick up my kids from school and be in my pj's at home, writing this book.

Give it a few seconds of gratitude. Open your heart to how it can work even bigger miracles in your life.

I'm going to take us through the big shifts I see women experience most often, but as you discover your blessings throughout this book, take some time and go ahead and write your answers right on the page. (Yes, that's legal! Please let this be your guide. Scribble away!) Your future self thanks you for the answers you find and write inside these pages. Someday, you'll come back to your answers; you'll reminisce and be amazed at how life has evolved. Let it be a chronicle of the true miracle you and your business teaming up can be.

I'm so excited for you.

I Didn't See It for Years

I've been in business since 2013. Ten years and three companies later, it finally dawned on me. My third business, The Juicy Good Life, was divinely sent to help me heal. I formed her in 2018, but it wasn't until an aha moment in 2023 that it became so incredibly clear.

I can still feel the tears start to form. This Word doc is getting blurry. My shoulders are curving inward, and I can feel the protective posture start.

I've taken my hands off the keyboard, a little frozen, twice already since starting to type. This is the power of the realization. It's tied up in all my trauma.

It turns out—literally everything in this business is a healing balm for me.

Then, it cascades out to my clients.

But it's my medicine first.

The name of my company?

The Juicy Good Life.

The vision of my company? To help heal the world one businesswoman at a time.

The mission of my company? Help reduce suffering and amplify joy.

My *why*? To bring more Love with a capital L to the world.

That aha in 2023? I'm here helping female business owners suffer less because I am the daughter of a business owner who I saw in constant suffering.

> Everything in this business is
> a healing balm for me.

I grew up helping customers from the time I could pull up a stool to run the cash register in a gift and floral store in the tiny town of Elbow Lake, Minnesota. My mom created a beautiful Main Street destination because she put her mind to it. A decorator, a seamstress, a florist, and a determined visionary. It was a success.

My mom had talent for days and physical misery for miles. She gave it her all. She could make everything beautiful—except her health. In between huge holiday shopping seasons, the weekend weddings, and constant funerals she'd do the flowers for—and raising two little kids while my dad worked all the time—she'd end up in the hospital again and again.

It got so bad that I started a "Care Club" with my little brother. Tanner was three years younger than me, but even at five and eight years old, we could be strategic. We'd meet in my closet and pre-make get well cards for my mom because we knew we'd need them.

But it wasn't just the hospitalizations for migraines and surgeries; it was the stress that came out sideways in my parents' marriage. The stress of working parents trying to do it all (they also created one of the most beautiful historic homes and yards in our little town) created chaos.

From my perspective now, life was the opposite of juicy good. It was a pressure cooker of business stress, relationship stress, and never-ending physical suffering. It took a toll on all of us. I have deep compassion for all the pain she went through.

> **Whatever it is that your business is here to help you heal, it's still very tender.**

I can't go back in time and change it for my mom, but I have changed it for me. I decided long ago, well before I finally saw the correlation between my business mission and my wounds, illness and pain would not be side effects of business stress. I want to take the positives I learned forward and heal the rest. I'm sure this is painful for my parents to reflect on too. I don't want to hurt anyone. My mom and dad did what they could with what they had to work with (which was a boatload of their own massive trauma). And, because of my deep compassion for my parents' pain, I believe it's my soul's imperative to make sure I got the memo and don't repeat the cycles of chaos in my life.

I'm shaking as I share this story even now, despite having a couple of years to integrate this realization. Because whatever it is that your business is here to help you heal, it's still very tender.

You might be having your aha already.

Be gentle. Go slowly. Regulate your nervous system with a soothing practice of some sort. It's no small potatoes, this realization.

You Don't Have to Force It

The cool thing about the change I've talked about so far is that you don't even have to consciously choose to heal as you grow your business. It happens as we go, as long as we don't numb it away (more on that later).

That's why I often say our businesses are "divinely sent" to help us heal. I was five years into my divinely sent, super obvious (not yet to me) business before it clicked as to what was really happening. The Juicy Good Life has already been healing me for years. Without me even trying.

The inspiration for what I wanted to create.
Healing me first.
The alignment with what I want to teach.
Healing me first.
The clients I get to coach.
Calling me up to my mission.
The money I get to create.
Expanding my vessel.

All of it has lined up for my higher good. That feels pretty darn divine.

My first two companies did the same—in much more hustle-tastic, stressful ways.

> **Your business is likely already healing you in ways you don't realize.**

Your business is likely already healing you in ways you don't realize. It's my intention to help you see it so you can awaken to even more blessings. Because when I realized my company was my medicine, I started to appreciate it in deep, profound ways. And my heart opened to how I could be the most healed version of myself through my business.

Because that version of me? She is able to handle way more joy.

And joy in business is magnetic to what you want in life.

Created for Purpose

Your Business Chose You

Your business chose you. It chose you so it could be born into the world through your vision. Does your heart expand when you think of it that way? Your business didn't drop into anyone else's lap.

That is a truly divine thing. Because only you could bring it into existence in the way it wants to help the world. You have the dream because you embody the recipe to make it real. And while that incredible inspiration is uniquely yours, this business will also push all your buttons in ways unique to you.

Both matter.

Both create momentum.

Inspiration keeps us in creative mode, and the button-pushing trigger side of our businesses keep us showing up to evolve. Creation and evolution are the gifts of this business growth experience.

When you take a 30,000-foot view of your business, it's fabulous to see what you have brought to the world.

You solve someone's problems.
You make someone's life more beautiful.
You are a collaborator in your customer's life.

....

> You have the dream because you
> embody the recipe to make it real.

....

Take a moment and reflect on what you've created from the inspiration to run your business.

What are you most proud of?

What didn't exist before you decided you'd make it a reality?

Who has been helped along the way?

How have you shown yourself and others what's possible?

If I know you, ten seconds of this reflection might feel like too long for your brain. Can I invite you to truly bask in your creation? Can you give yourself a good twenty seconds?

Hold up, it's only been five seconds. Did you answer those questions?

(I'm smiling because I see you.)

....

> Creation and evolution are the gifts of
> this business growth experience.

....

One of the most beautiful exercises I have ever done was writing a love letter to my business.[1] (Thank you, Nicole Lewis-Keeber, for that gift of an idea.) This may be a great time to think about writing one to your business. Whether you write one or not, this appreciation spark is the beginning of creating a relationship with a business that loves you back.

A LOVE LETTER TO MY BUSINESS:

Your Business Chose You

Worth the Squirm

Your Why

As we continue to build the evidence that your business can be a powerful advocate of the life you want to live, hopefully, you're already feeling inspired and amazed at what your beautiful business can do for you.

Let's lean into how healing your *why* can be. You know, that WHY that Simon Sinek made a popular concept so many years ago.[2] It's the reason you do what you do.

If you're a giver, like so many women who are drawn to my work, you are typically going to start with an outward reason.

Your kids.

Your community.

Your customers.

The planet.

Your legacy.

Maybe it was to escape corporate baloney. Maybe your why started as a "have to make something work" because of a layoff or life change.

Your answer is exactly where we start. That is surface level. But let's dig deeper.

Look at your why (find it now) and feel free to write it here to help anchor it in.

....

Lean into how healing your *why* can be.

....

My why:

When I think of my why when I got into business, it was because my little boy, who was two years old at the time, started having major meltdowns at bedtime when he was in daycare.

My husband and I were TV news co-anchors for the local NBC station in our city. That meant both Mom and Dad worked from 2:00 p.m. to about 11:00 p.m. every night. Our babies were in second-shift daycare.

Of course, there aren't as many kiddos in daycare at that time of night, so the daycare staff would combine age groups after the big pickup rush at 5:30 p.m. Our little dude did okay until it was bedtime. Then the "big boys" (who were up to age twelve or so) were way more energetic than a toddler who needed to settle down.

He had just graduated from the baby room, where his sister was snuggled in. (I would go nurse Kaydie to sleep on my dinner break, and my husband and I would play with Kanyon until we had to go back.) He was out of his element, and he was scared.

It didn't matter what we tried—he would panic every night around 8:00 p.m. While I was preparing for our 9:00 and 10:00 p.m. newscasts, if I dared peek at the daycare webcam, I would witness a heartbreaking scene that is still seared into my memory all these years later.

My sweet little baby boy would be at the half-door of his daycare room, pulling on it with all his might, crying his eyes out, his little body shaking with the upset of feeling scared to go to bed.

He wanted Mama and Daddy. He wanted home. He wanted his quiet nest.

I'm bawling just recounting it, as it was such a catalyst for me to wake up and change. You see, I loved my career. I'd spent nearly two decades devoting myself to news, and I always saw myself retiring from the anchor desk.

But this was too much suffering for my sweetheart. My mama heart couldn't take it. My husband did everything he could, and my mom tried to help, but this was uncharted territory for us. We knew that this was not how we wanted our child to live Monday through Friday. And truly, in a few short years, once they were in school, we'd never see them because of our evening shift.

We made a decision.

One of us would have to leave.

We made a pros and cons list in our living room. I can still remember that big piece of white paper hanging up with painter's tape on our picture window.

The list was pretty evenly split. I had two things that swung the pendulum to having me leave TV. One, I was confident I could run a business, and two, I was still the food source for our baby girl.

So, I left.

Three incredible companies and a lot of learning later, I now understand it sometimes takes painful circumstances to get us to do scary things like leave a career you love to launch a business.

I would tell the story of my why being my kids for more than a decade. But now I know it was the catalyst. It's not my why anymore.

>   May you allow what your business
>   growth wants to show you too.

My business evolution (from owning a women's magazine to creating a global marketing agency to becoming a business coach for women) has revealed to me that while doing it for my kids is noble and easily co-signed by anyone who hears that story, it's so much deeper.

Each chapter in this book serves as its own healing guide for me as well. I knew it would, but I continue to be surprised by the new layers revealed to me.

May you allow what your business growth wants to show you too. Let the aha moments roll in. Just yesterday, as I prepared to draft this chapter on how our why is healing, this is the procrastination social media post I was inspired to write:

> I'm here to reduce suffering and amplify joy.
>
> Why?
>
> I saw a talented and hardworking set of parents live in crisis and chaos, and it made my life hell as a kid.
>
> Everything had to look good from the road: perfect house, perfect children, perfect work ethic. Inside: stress. Illness. Fear. Flinching. Abuse. Screaming. Fighting.
>
> Looking back, it was a total WTF.
>
> It taught me to be judgment-proof. The achiever who could stay ahead of the chaos through climbing ladders.
>
> That led to burnout and losing myself. Hell, I hadn't even found her yet.
>
> Because I wanted to (and had to feed my family) grow my business, I embarked on a pretty cool adventure to find me.
>
> I love her.
>
> I used to admire her.

> But now I actually know her.
> And I love her.

Oof.

Even as I think I have everything figured out, a new insight comes.

So yes, my why to get into business ownership was for the sake of my sweet toddler's well-being. But my business path has helped me heal so much that I can now see the deeper and divine wisdom at play back then. The deep desire for my baby to feel safe and held. My inner child needs it too.

A healed mama is a ripple for every child she raises.

A healed woman is one step closer to a healed world.

....

**A healed woman is one step
closer to a healed world.**

....

My why now is being absolutely okay with healing me. It's how everything else gets done. It's how I can show up grounded and holding powerful space for my clients and my family and my community. It's everything.

A healing me, a healing you . . .

We make more calm, loving choices. We learn to regulate our nervous systems. We can meet challenges with new solutions. This interrupts generational trauma patterns. This is medicine for all.

Your Business Name

As I coached more and more small business founders, I discovered something fun and super helpful. On the macro level, as we look at how our business is here to be a conduit for our healing and becoming more true to ourselves (which is one and the same in my mind), sometimes that medicine is right under our noses.

In the name of our business!

Think about it for a moment.

What we name our business is typically guided by inspiration, which I think is our soul speaking. The meaning of our company's name is usually our very own recipe for life.

Take "The Juicy Good Life" as an easy example. At the time I was founding it, I took the results I wanted my clients to experience and added some pizzazz. Some "juice," you could say.

I didn't want your life to be just good. Too basic. Not visceral enough.

I wanted you to get the result of a life that is so fantastic, you can call it juicy good!

> **I wanted you to get the result of a life that is so fantastic, you can call it juicy good!**

As it turns out, that is exactly what I need too. But my brain was so busy getting geared up to serve clients as a business coach that I didn't see the delicious insight for myself until many years into my practice.

By now, I'm sure you're already poring over your name and running it through the filter of belief (or disregard), and that's the point.

Think about the name of your business. Now, think about how that is here for YOU.

How is it a guide for you?

How could it help you show up more fully?

How does it embody the ways you want to help the world?

How could it call you forward in your leadership?

How can it help you be in alignment with the results you want your customers to experience?

I have a client who advocates for parents as they learn to feed their babies. Often, these new moms come to her at the end of their rope, with painful and scary scenarios unfolding. Some of these parents are afraid they will have to settle and feed their babies in ways they didn't anticipate. Some are getting unhelpful information that leads to even more pain and difficulties.

Guess what she named her company? Mama Bear Family Care.

How perfect of a guiding light is that name for her? It's truly a compass when she needs to tap into that fierce advocate part of her, which is not easy, but it sure embodies how she shows up to protect those "cubs" and their parents. She is also gentle and playful in her business, hosting fun gatherings and building community. And when her clients need her, she is a steady, compassionate presence.

When Jennifer, the owner of Mama Bear Family Care, needs inspiration, she has learned to look to the very roots of her business, printed in vinyl on the front door of her office and on every business card. You can too.

> **When she gets back into alignment with the heart and the soul, it helps her filter through any confusion and creates clarity.**

Danielle named her boutique Heart & Soul Home Decor. She launched this business as a passion project with her teenage daughter. It's also a nod to how much she loved making memories with her grandma. Both generations of women she loves light up her heart and soul. She was willing to make a big change and sell her first business to devote her time to the company that makes her heart and soul happy.

If she's moving through a decision and I'm coaching her on it, you can bet there will be a moment when I ask her what it is she wants the spirit of her business to show her. She often goes back to wanting everyone to have that "Christmas morning feeling" in their homes all year round.

When she gets back into alignment with the heart and the soul, it helps her filter through any confusion and creates clarity. She tunes in and weighs the options, checking to see which one will help her feel like she's coming down the stairs to all the twinkling lights. It only takes a moment for her to make aligned decisions.

Go back to your inspired business name. It doesn't have to be super deep.

Maybe you named your company after yourself. Guess what? That totally works too. This is the business of coming home to your truth. My second company was comprised of my last name and my husband's last name. Stokes Herzog Marketing and Consulting isn't as profound when you're putting it through a healing lens as I'm doing in this chapter, but it was a guidepost.

> Our logos and taglines can also help us rise up to who we're meant to be.

You know what we (the Stokes and the Herzog in this scenario) had to get really good at? Marketing and consulting. And we did. It was simple, and so was our priority in feeding the big machine we built. We had to market and consult to keep the engines going. Our name made our marching orders clear as day. Looking back, it also helped heal the Stokes and the Herzog involved. More on that later.

Our logos and taglines can also help us rise up to who we're meant to be. Even a business named for its region for practicality's sake can look to its tagline for this healing inspiration. Let's just make up one to bring home the point:

West Field Pet Supply

Where fur babies come first.

This is likely a company started from a love of pets. To drill deeper, I imagine this person feels a certain amount of joy from having a fur baby. That joy matters, and when they use it to guide their business-building, they will find it to be much more sustainable.

If I'm coaching this person and they stray from their tagline—by focusing on profit margins to the detriment of the well-being of the pets they serve—they are NOT likely going to see the results they want in their business. They may accidentally knock themselves out of alignment.

When we profess a tagline, energetically, it matters that we line up with living it.

If you're like me, you have a few offers you've named inside your business too. They can be a compass without you even realizing what's going on. It's truly the best. Have some fun with it!

I am almost giggling at myself that I didn't see it, but my first intense coaching, mastermind, and scaling offer was called "All In." This inspiration came to me while I was very much still the CEO and hands-on owner of our marketing agency.

All In was an intense, year-long program that helped incredible women do incredible things. They went all in. Just like the name invited them to do.

You already see it coming, don't ya?

But I didn't. Until year two of All In. I very much wanted to be all in on The Juicy Good Life company. I had so many obligations and responsibilities in my marketing agency, the pressure to prioritize the agency was all-consuming for the better part of a decade. The All In program gave me the first "Duh, Sarah" opportunity to look at what I was being led to do. It was time for me to follow the divine guidance. And I did.

Then came Should Free Six Figures.

I developed it as I needed its very message for myself. I was in the process of de-shoulding the entire scope of my entrepreneurship. The name came before I even realized the powerful impact it would have on my life. I was de-shoulding right alongside the women who signed up to be founders of the program.

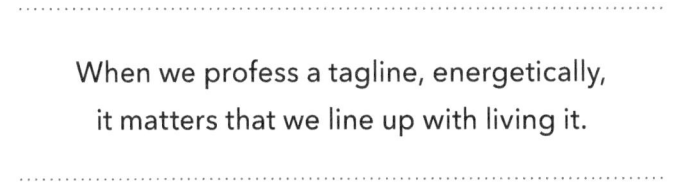

When we profess a tagline, energetically, it matters that we line up with living it.

(Spoiler alert, I did end up going Should Free and All In on my coaching company, and it was the best thing I've done so far career-wise.)

How is your business name, logo, tagline, or offer name a guide for you?

How could it help you show up more fully?

How does it embody the ways you want to help the world?

How could it call you forward in your leadership?

Your Mission, Vision, and Values

Just as with the name you choose for your company and your why, you can look to your mission, vision, and values for a map that will help you evolve. If you've never created the mission, vision, and values for your company, not to worry. They are likely already there, running in the background. All you have to do is look at how you show up and what you care about as you operate your business.

I can simplify this a bunch for you. We often think this must be some grandiose process that takes 743 meetings (especially if you come from corporate).

The **vision** is that big dream and hope for the change you can make.

The **mission** is the *how* you get there.

The **values** are the ways you want to show up daily.

Think about **vision** in terms of the long-term impact you dream of making.

Think about **mission** as the core ingredients to get there.

Think about **values** as your behavior along the way.

When I declared mine six years ago, I didn't have the dots connected on how my business would help me heal, so I didn't see how profound the mission, vision, and values would be. I wanted to do business "right," and The Juicy Good Life was my third company. She was my passion project. Not something I *had* to start—something I was inspired to start.

For the first time in my five years of entrepreneurship, I wasn't in survival mode, building the airplane as I flew it. I wanted to set myself up with a mission, vision, and values statement first. I got to be fancy like that. I had the runway to launch, a team to create the brand pieces, and the luxury of time before takeoff.

> **What we think will be inspiring for the people we help is here for us first.**

I sat myself down in my corner office inside our marketing agency and started to craft the powerful guideposts for my biggest evolution yet. Admittedly, it wasn't as profound as it sounds. I was getting these declared so I could check the box of having it ready for my team member who wanted to put it on the website. (We were all very big box-checkers in our agency life.)

I asked myself, "What is it I'm trying to do here?"

I created The Juicy Good Life because I was looking for a role model and mentor. I looked around and didn't find anyone like me who wanted to change the world while being a great mom, kick-butt businesswoman, and be in her pajamas napping a lot too.

I cared about changing the world. I gave a dang about businesswomen loving life more and experiencing success without all the stress. I wanted to focus on growth, joy, and being a business owner who could keep her heart wide open.

My heart was in the right place, of course, but as I reflect six years later, I want to tell her, "Oh, Sarah, you have no idea how big of an order form you're putting into the universe for yourself right now."

That order form:

> Mission: Reduce suffering; amplify joy.
> Vision: Help heal the world, one businesswoman at a time.
> Values: Open-hearted, growth-minded, authentic joy.

What we think will be inspiring for the people we help is here for us **first**. A compass for how to show up in order to align with your divinely sent company.

If I'm not reducing suffering and amplifying joy in my own work and personal life, I'm not likely going to resonate with clients in my coaching, marketing, and sales the way I want.

Our mission is our map. It's not just what we want for our clients; it's the secret code to being magnetic. When we embody our mission and let it be our central guide, we are unstoppable.

This is one of the best hacks ever. Think about the mission of your business and apply it to your life and leadership. If YOU are not yet actively benefiting from your mission, you might feel out of harmony with your business.

Let your mission be your map.

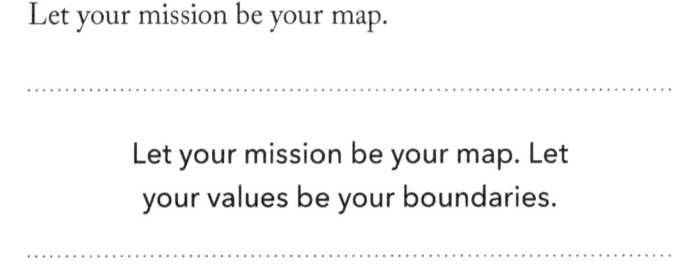

Let your values be your boundaries.
Katie Rubin taught me that "our values show us our boundaries." And from Mary Brown, boundaries coach, I learned that boundaries are what we are available for and what we are not available for.

If I'm not being open-hearted, that's going to show up in my energy levels and revenue. If I'm not taking a growth-minded approach when I lead my company, I'm probably not inspired and will lose inertia. If I'm not making room for authentic joy or just doing what I think *should* make me happy, I'm out of alignment—period.

I believe alignment is when our actions match our values. That when we show up in life as a match to what we say is most important to us, life flows better. The same goes for doing business.

That's the biggest takeaway here.

Have you ever noticed when you are out of whack as you try to lead? When you don't feel that trust in your decisions, or that marketing isn't clicking, or you are running into customers who don't value what you do? Those times when you question if you have what it takes or if you even want to keep going?

You've likely strayed from your own built-in compass.

Each spring, I take women through the exercise of getting clarity on their mission, vision, and values during my strategic planning retreat called Cultivate. Last year, one of my clients realized "slow living" was one of her business values. For her, it meant that relaxed feeling of being on the back deck, under the patio lights, having a beverage with friends. (Cool, right? If you knew her, you would want to be on that back deck enjoying her effervescence too.) She knew exactly what that value would look and feel like in her business. And by declaring this one value, she has the power to prevent burnout.

> I believe alignment is when our actions match our values.

It's a critical tool for an achiever who wants to savor life. When the hurried energy of the business world is tempting, she will find her most incredible insight and sustainable growth if she gives herself the gift of slow living.

I smile when I imagine the benefits to her nervous system. She's a projector (Human Design) and is learning how to rest.[3] That's one of the keys to how her life will flow more easily. The benefits to her creativity are immense, as she's known for her fabulous marketing messages that you can tell were not cranked out in a rush. In a world that tells you to hurry, slow living is a value that will serve her so well.

Another client declared education to be one of her values. She embodies it naturally because she's so passionate about her products and loves to help people understand why she carefully selects certain ingredients and the ways they will relieve pain for her customers. But getting to know her past, she's healing from big challenges as a girl who was homeschooled and dealt with dyslexia yet persevered against all odds to get into college and become a doctor.

When she chose education as a main value for her company, she probably didn't realize how powerful that dedication to learning is. She actively decided that education would play a key role in changing her young life, and it guides her still today as she leads her company.

> Let your values show you your boundaries.
> Let your vision light your fire.

I imagine that if someone wanted to collaborate with her but didn't want to hear about the amazing aspects of her formulas and why she uses the ingredients she does, she would feel off. One of her core values wouldn't be honored, and over time, that would be corrosive to her experience with them.

Let your values show you your boundaries.

Let your vision light your fire.

Goodness knows, we all get to points in our business where we're down in the dumps and don't have that same fire in our belly. This is where our vision can act as a spark. To help you remember why you're willing to do all this heavy lifting in the first place. Your vision, even if you don't realize what it is yet, is the thing that can be rocket fuel.

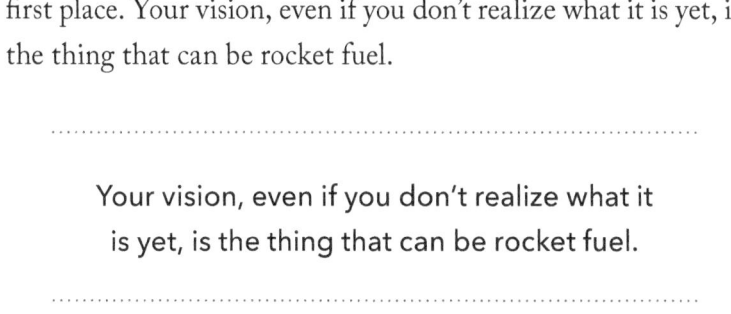

So many of us had a career before we owned a business. We're used to seeing companies declare a vision, maybe put it on a plaque in the breakroom or conference room, but you may have felt removed from it or didn't see management focus on anything but those daily fires everyone needed to put out.

Heck, as a scaling marketing agency owner, I was so busy firefighting that I didn't even create a vision statement for years. We had a tagline that drove us, and it was enough at the time. "Trusted names building trusted brands" was the tagline, and we did just that. Ours included. We built our own trusted brands as we built the brands of our clients. It did light my fire. I loved the achievement of it all, but it wouldn't be the long-lasting impact that would bring me to joyful tears.

That comes from my vision for The Juicy Good Life. The idea of helping heal the world one businesswoman at a time keeps me going through the squirm for sure. Number one, now that I see it's healing *this* businesswoman first, I have come far enough on my spiritual journey to realize that would be enough. That would create enough of a ripple for me to leave this earth knowing I had done my healing so my kids and their kids wouldn't have to heal the same old wounds. They end with me. That would be plenty of impact.

We're always healing through our businesses, and therefore, we help heal the world too.

But this vision keeps me going because as a nurturer and helper, most days, it's easier to show up for my clients than myself. That lights my fire for sure. Whether it is a client with a dream I can help accelerate or a client in tears because her spouse isn't being supportive, I kick into go mode. Six years in, I know it's a parallel process. When I heal this business owner, I can be in even better shape to help you. We're always healing through our businesses, and therefore, we help heal the world too. Totally worth the squirm.

The Results We Want

If I only had one page to get this message across, this would be the page. The results you want for your customers? That is your medicine, first and always.

You've heard the "We teach what we need" saying, right? That's the gist. Only so many business owners don't realize yet that we can flip that to "We sell what we need," and we could all get the aha right now.

Maybe your brain is already protesting, "But, Sarah, I sell fertilizer. I don't need fertilizer as medicine for me!" The results you want go much deeper than you think, even if you sell a product. Ah, welcome to my sales masterclass too.

Me: Why do you sell fertilizer, Suzie Q?

Suzie Q: I want people's gardens to grow!

Me: Why do you want people's gardens to grow?

Suzie Q: So they are happy, proud of their garden, and can feed their family well.

Me: Why do you want them to be happy and feed their family?

Suzie Q: Because it takes the stress and worry off her shoulders.

Me: Boom.

Suzie Q: Ohhhhhhhh.

Suzie's is selling stress and worry relief. As a side bonus, she's selling happiness and a sense of pride too.

This is her medicine.

I can bet that Susie, our fictional friend, needs relief from stress and worry. She wants happiness and a sense of pride. So many of us get there by choosing to help others get it through our businesses.

> **So many of us get there by choosing to help others get it through our businesses.**

I have a client who paints beautiful murals on the sides of buildings. On the surface, we could say her results are to add beauty to the world. That would be plenty fabulous. But I remember seeing the sparkle in her eye at a workshop when she connected with a deeper meaning behind the murals. She was thinking about why a business owner would want to commission a mural and invest in her art. She started with it being a tourism draw. Yes, that is absolutely a return on investment and a wonderful marketing angle.

Then she dug deeper when I asked why someone would want to draw in tourists (aside from the tourism dollars), and she got it. "It helps them connect with their community," she realized. It was a really cool moment. Think of that business owner with a beautiful mural on their building—how much that could be a conversation starter and how much joy it can bring.

> She absolutely glows when she's sharing her art with people. So do her clients.

From that realization on, I saw her show up with new insight. That would be enough of a benefit to last her the rest of her business ownership days. But to see *her* in action is to know that she shines brightest when she, too, connects with her community through art. She absolutely glows when she's sharing her art with people. So do her clients. It's her medicine and their delightful results.

I just had coffee with a friend and introduced her to this concept. She was feeling like she wanted to take her business to new levels but had some confusion and overwhelm going on.

I asked her what results she wants for her customers. It was so lovely. She said she wants her customers to learn about wellness, live a life that feels clean, and to have a joyful time.

As she spoke about it, she mentioned the word clean and joy so much, it might as well have been on a neon sign. I said, "It sounds like clean joy is your medicine, first." She lit up. That was the resonance she was looking for. I told her she could use clean joy as her filter for big decisions she has coming up in her life. It clicked. You could see the melt of relief on her face and in her shoulders.

She had a new way to let her soul guide her through the squirm. And you know what's absolutely amazing? Later that day, I got to visit her store. As she showed me around her product line, she looked at me with a smile. The name of her wellness line? It's the Norwegian word for clean! You cannot make this stuff up. I go into full geek-out mode on this one.

This is similar to your *why* but brings a new angle to it. Our why keeps us getting out of bed for this business thing we do. Even when it's hard.

> **Our why keeps us getting out of bed for this business thing we do. Even when it's hard.**

The concept of the results we want for our customers being our medicine first? This keeps us evolving through a deep connection to ourselves. It can bring us back into alignment on the days we feel off-kilter. It keeps us nourished and guided, not just getting out of bed and going through the motions.

When I feel like I'm doing it wrong, I come back to the very thing I want for my beloved clients. My answer to every question starts with, "What reduces my suffering and amplifies my joy?" When I am anchored in this alignment actively making moves that reduce my suffering and amplify my joy, I am magnetic. You will be too. Your turn.

The results I want for my customers:

Now, identify the key words that stand out to you. Boil it down to just a few words or a powerful phrase:

How does this result(s) help me in my life first?

Designed for Connection

It Kicks Up All of Our Stuff

If you think about it, our business will eventually kick up all of our stuff. Literally, everything that wants to be healed and loved on will come up for your review. If you want to grow your business, you are in for the biggest personal growth adventure of your life. But it's not a bad thing!

Squirmy? Oh yeah.

Remember back to the first pages of this book when I invited you to think of your business as your best friend, a powerful healing partner, a soul guide, etc.? Welcome that perspective back to the front of your mind as you consider these chapters. Our business growth adventure will bring us face-to-face with all the most impactful facets of life. This is where we will get to decide again and again how we want to show up.

It calls us up, not calls us out. Being called out is punitive. Being called up is loving. Like a mentor who believes in you. They know you can do it. So does your business. Because it's a benevolent energy.

> Our business growth adventure will bring us face-to-face with all the most impactful facets of life.

Your business is not the enemy that needs conquering. It calls you up to be in connection with your true self. It wants you to express your bright, shining, talented soul.

It chose you.

It wants the best for you.

And it wants to be right by your side as you build.

Numb It or Heal It

As a student of Dr. Brené Brown's work (I'm a Dare to Lead trained professional), I have learned that we have a few choices when it comes to the squirm of growth I'm talking about.

We can numb it, we can heal it, or we can muddle through a bit of both. That's where I find my very human-y self, most days. When the stuff hits the fan in life, I'm definitely going to show up and do my inner work to get the lesson, but I might be elbow-deep in Cool Ranch Doritos while I do it.

Numbing is what Brené (can we be on a first-name basis, here? Hoping my editor will let this stay—because I totally call her Brené instead of Dr. Brown) uses to describe the way we try to escape the hard feelings. Numbing can be buying every dress Instagram sends you an ad for (ask me how I know), drinking a glass of wine, mindlessly scrolling social media, eating our feelings, gossiping, bingeing a season of *Emily in Paris*, or even starting a fight with your partner.

Anything that takes us away from the actual work of being with ourselves as we process the tough stuff (aka being in the squirm) is numbing. We've probably had our numbing of choice embedded for years, if not decades. Numbing is a short-term escape hatch, but being able to love yourself as you squirm and grow has a long-lasting grounding effect. It will not feel good at all in the beginning. But the more we set down the Doritos and love ourselves, the more expansive we become.

When we decide we want to grow our business, we also sign up for squirming.

When we decide we want to grow our business, we also sign up for squirming. The more we numb to avoid the squirm, the longer our painful patterns stick around.

One of my clients used to talk about how she would "go into the tank." This would be distressing for her and disruptive for her life because she beat herself up emotionally for needing this time-out. It makes total sense why she ended up in the "tank." This would look like needing to be in bed, getting sick, and not having the capacity to show up for her work or family the way she wanted. Her body, mind, and spirit were begging for her to take a beat and give herself what she needed as she grew her business and healed her trauma.

She wasn't numbing with nacho chips; she wasn't numbing with wine. Her numbing looked a lot like being numb to her needs. After working with her for many months, we saw how pushing through her internal cues for replenishment was landing her in full depletion. This depletion felt like a constant setback for her. But as over-givers, my clients don't even realize how much they are trying to pour from an empty pitcher until their body begs for help.

We began to ask a simple question that you can ask yourself: *What do I need right now?*

For her, she wanted way more grounding. Spending time with trees. Taking walks even when her to-do list was long. Being with her sweet pup. Having a slow ramp-up to the week. Getting help with her paperwork. It was journaling and giving a voice to the parts of her that wanted connection. It was getting weekly therapy, doing parts work with a professional.[4]

She really showed up for herself during the squirms. She got coaching every time she was wobbly and kept asking herself the powerful question. But better yet, she didn't just ask the question (what do I need?). She started to give herself what she needed. One slow Monday at a time. One loving conversation to help her husband understand her evolution at a time. One hug of a tree at a time. She began to give herself the incredible attention she so easily showers on her clients.

The beautiful thing is, I haven't heard her say, "I went into the tank," for a couple of years now. Now she speaks so much more kindly about getting her needs met. (Cue my grateful tears.) Her business has grown right alongside her squirm. The relief comes from not trying to outrun our squirm but to incorporate it as a sacred messenger.

The next time you find yourself in your favorite numbing mechanism, what would it be like to gently get curious? *What do I need right now?*

Then give it to yourself.

Even if it is the bag of chips, good news, you are no longer detached from your needs, unconsciously numbing. Now you are at a choice point. You get to choose how you cope. That is okay. And that is enough. One day, your coping will be way more supportive than it may be today.

> **Every time we wake up to our needs, we heal a bit.**

The beautiful bonus is that you've loved yourself more by asking the question. This is progress. Eventually, you'll choose to love yourself through the squirm without the old crutches you used to rely on.

Every time we wake up to our needs, we heal a bit. The next squirm becomes less daunting. Perfection is not required. Awareness is.

When we proactively tune in to what we need, we do our business and our bodies the biggest favor. You are the most valuable asset in your business. Tending to yourself is proactive business growth of the highest form.

Ninety Seconds or Ninety Years

We know growing our business and simultaneously just being a human living on Planet Earth right now is fertile ground for being in fight, flight, or freeze all day, every day.

From cash flow to politics, all you have to do is touch the screen of your phone, and we can dive head-first into things that press all of our touchy buttons.

And that's before you even have your first cup of coffee.

Depending on your season of business and life, you could face all the things that activate your nervous system even before lunch.

Being a human who's building a business is full of opportunities to freak out. To overthink. To struggle. To shame and blame yourself.

I see business owners show up with their preferred method of coping in a few different ways. Some of us do what Brené

Brown calls over-functioning. We hop in and fix everything for everyone. We take action—in full slay-the-day mode.

> **Being a human who's building a business is full of opportunities to freak out.**

Some business owners are frozen in the squirm—in a stressful mix of nervous system activation, trauma responses, and limiting beliefs. You don't have to look further than your nearest social media group for female entrepreneurs to see this in every plea-for-help post. Stay in either of these stress responses too long, and we will meet up with unintended consequences.

Sometimes I'll meet business owners who are convinced the grind is the answer. They tell me in private that they want to see their kids more, and they want to feel relaxed and take time off, but they are not ready to break up with the busy badge. I understand. I couldn't break up with mine until I started hallucinating in my kitchen while I pulled yet another all-nighter to get my magazine done while still trying to keep all the other plates spinning too.

The culture of hustle totally co-signs on trying to outrun your feelings. Just throw yourself into action, and you can avoid feeling discomfort. You'll be too distracted to notice what your body, mind, and spirit want you to pay attention to.

I loved my "busy badge" so much. It gave me all the gold stars my achievement-addicted self needed. After many years of healing and doing parts work, I now understand why I chose achievement and perfectionism as my preferred numbing methods (along with food). It was the way I got my needs met. Instead of beating myself up for years of hustle and grind, I thank past me for showing me what I don't want to do again. She took care of me in the only ways she knew how at the time.

....

The culture of hustle totally co-signs on trying to outrun your feelings.

....

But the breakup with the busy badge can't be just glossed over in a paragraph. It took literal YEARS of deconditioning from getting applause for being the hardest worker. I had to learn and discover for myself two things. They make a great case for getting comfy with the squirm of unlearning our old coping strategies. They are the most powerful messages I've heard.

I knew from experience that *if you don't listen to your body's whispers, you will end up hearing it scream*. I could see it from my childhood. My mom's body paid the price. I see entrepreneurial women throw their backs out, get super sick, and even end up getting injured before they take a break.

We call that the "two-by-four" from the universe. And if you get those, because we all do, you haven't done anything wrong. You are not to blame for the stuff that goes haywire. There are messages in every painful circumstance.

> There are messages in every painful circumstance.

I care enough about your well-being to risk someone thinking I'm victim-blaming here. I'm asking you to see my intention of shining a light on where we can love ourselves better. Not all ailments or flat tires are caused by not listening. Sometimes it's just a time-out to rest.

Sometimes our kid brings the virus home.

Sometimes it's a leaky valve stem.

And sometimes, which is my invitation here, it IS a red flag asking you to pay attention. We're here to learn the difference. We cannot see it until we see it.

I had my own two-by-fours, of course, in addition to hallucinating in my kitchen (happened twice from exhaustion). When I would overbook myself instead of just saying no, I'd end up with a bad headache or migraine, or even a problem with my car. I knew what was happening. I'd ignored the whispers or missed the memos and overextended. I promised myself somewhere along the line that I would catch my whispers faster. It helped that my spiritual mentor, Aveen, and my life coach, Jodi, were very clear on how our body talks to us.

My friends are probably sick of me saying out loud, "I got the memo!" to the universe. I do it every time I smell a two-by-four or an illness coming. I name it out loud, letting my divine support team know I do NOT need a nudge. It matters to me that I don't needlessly suffer anymore. That doesn't mean I'm not still tempted to continue overbooking myself, because my trauma response (people pleaser) is loud when I think about saying no to someone.

Sparing my body or my vehicle the two-by-four? It's worth the squirm of deconditioning from saying a yes when it was really no. It's worth the squirm of being judged for resting instead of grinding out one more whatever we think we have to do.

Where do you abandon yourself and pay the price?

Where do you abandon yourself and pay the price?

(EEK! That feels harsh, but I'm here to help you, so I'll get uncomfy.)

The other lesson that really helped me embrace the squirm was a much more reassuring concept than the two-by-four. It's that *our most intense emotions don't last more than ninety seconds at their peak.* So, that fear, disappointment, rage, whatever we've been outrunning—it will be loudest for just a minute and a half.

Now, if you've ever grieved the loss of someone close to you, you probably already want to scream at this. I understand. You don't have to pretend your grief only lasts ninety seconds. You don't have to apply this to grief. In fact, please don't. Let that process be what it needs to be. Keep reading for what it means about our brain chemicals and triggers.

This is a concept for the daily squirms our businesses bring up. The speaking opportunity we avoid. The sale we don't make because it felt safer to barter. The delegation request we don't follow through on because it will be faster just to do it ourselves.

The stuff that feels really triggering (brings up a painful memory or reflex) can stifle us so much that we may never show up in the way we want to, make the money we want to make, help the people we want to help, break the patterns we want to break—because we are hoping to outrun a ninety-second intense emotion.

Dr. Jill Bolte Taylor, a Harvard neuroscientist (she was made famous in her Ted Talk called "My Stroke of Insight"), explains that when something triggers us, our brain releases chemicals that create our emotions, but the chemical dissipates on its own within ninety seconds. If we continue to feel intense emotions after the ninety seconds, it is our thoughts about the trigger that fan the emotional flames.[5]

> **Our nervous system would much rather have us avoid triggers for ninety years than feel a feeling for ninety seconds.**

Our nervous system would much rather have us avoid triggers for ninety years than feel a feeling for ninety seconds. But the only way we can do that is to stay numb. I don't know about you, but numb isn't my life goal. All the joy I want to make room for is on the other side of that squirm.

This gives me comfort. I have decided to befriend my most intense emotions. This lady didn't even know she had rage living inside her because it was pushed so far down, it couldn't even see four seconds of daylight, much less ninety. I've slowly gained the capacity to notice, name, and let myself feel all kinds of emotions. If you would have met me ten years ago, you'd probably see me as a woman with a handful of emotions, all very pleasant, socially acceptable, and helpful. Now, I can access all kinds of feelings without needing to dive head-first into sugar and carbs. (I did this with the help of my coaches, healing therapies, and trusted friends who were safe witnesses to all my pain.) The best part is, when we can allow more of our real feelings to bubble up, we learn how to better access the incredible positive emotions we also want to feel.

My heart swells when I see clients take down the walls and let themselves feel whatever it is they are feeling. I know they are saving so much lifeforce when they let the tears fall or when they let themselves be pissed or resistant. It's all here to be felt, welcomed, and accepted as one more piece of our beautiful puzzle of being human.

This will be a practice. If you've found yourself saying, "If I cry, I'm afraid I'll never stop," or "I don't want to be mad," or "I shouldn't be so sad," my love—

Let.

Yourself.

Have.

That.

Feeling.

Remember, ninety seconds or ninety years? Let the feeling have its moment. Let's not get a migraine. Say the no you need to say and love yourself through the squirm of it. The alternative is to show up annoyed and resentful.

This is powerful stuff. You no longer need two-by-fours. You have a tool.

What whispers might you be getting?

What do those whispers want you to know?

What do you avoid so you don't have to feel ninety seconds of intense emotion?

What thoughts do you have that keep the intense emotions going longer than the ninety seconds?

Actors in Our Play

Our business will bring all kinds of people into our lives. Each one has a helpful role to play. Even the ones who are a pain in the rear.

A spiritual teacher of mine, Katie Rubin, reminded me that every human in our lives is an actor in our play. Oh, this has come in so handy when I am navigating challenging personalities. I also use it weekly with my clients who are going through a similar squirm in their business.

These actors in our play show us something. They act as mirrors so we can see what we need to see. Most of the time, they will be mirrors of fantastic validation that what we are doing matters. A sign someone out there benefits from our work. That our business matters.

Sometimes these actors in our play come into our lives to create friction. If nothing ever bugged you or went wrong in business, you'd likely never adapt or uncover new layers of who you are. There would be no friction to drive new clarity.

I'm thinking of one of the most ambitious humans I've ever met. She has dreams and goes for them. Her visions are easy to cheer on because they have a cool factor. Along the way, through multiple ventures, I've watched from afar as something goes haywire, then she gets torn to absolute shreds online. It's a pattern. Her business decisions continue to lead to highly charged and hurtful scenarios where she's dragged through the mud of criticism online. Commenters unleash. It's awful to witness, and I'm sure horrendous for her to experience.

If I were coaching her, instead of throwing our hands up and saying, "People are just jerks!" I'd want to get curious instead of getting furious. I've seen it happen enough times that at this point, my question would be: What wants to be felt and healed? (I am not excusing bad behavior via online trolls, and I fully disagree with that as a means to get messages across.) This is about the repeated pain and suffering this visionary goes through. What are these actors in her play here to show her? What feelings want to be witnessed? What compassion is called upon? What parts of her want connection?

Actors in our play will perform every role that a human holds in our business growth. They will come in every variation you can think of and typically in a way that helps you grow in your leadership.

It might present like one of these:

A parent with opinions.

A spouse with fear.

A sister with envy.

A client who doesn't pay you.

A colleague who seems like competition.

A vendor who doesn't follow through.

A team member who complains or takes advantage of your kindness.

> **Each challenging human in your business is a call on your leadership.**

Each challenging human in your business is a call on your leadership. It might lead you to therapy. It might lead you to new boundaries you need to set to protect your peace. It might lead you to new levels of courage and belief in yourself.

The next time you find yourself in a challenging situation with a human, ask yourself:

What story am I telling myself about this?

Is it a threat to my safety?

Where have I given their opinion too much power over me?

Would I make this person my CEO? (If not, we don't need to consider their input on our business.)

Would I want to trade places with this person?

Where are my values not being honored?

What boundary is this prompting me to set?

Where am I not honoring existing boundaries?

What solution is actually in my control here?

How would my most healed, courageous self want me to handle this?

Our Customers and Clients

I n the lifespan of our business, we will be lucky enough to meet some incredible customers and clients. Some will come into our lives and stay for years, being a dream come true, and some will be one-and-done. Finally, some will be lessons.

We will see all our beliefs and behaviors mirrored to us. That may feel really great most of the time, and we might bump our noses a few times as well. It all helps us get more clarity and courage to build a company that attracts incredible humans who love to pay you.

Think of a client you adore helping. You each do your part (you show up fully for what you promise to deliver; they show up and pay you). How do you feel when you work with them? Excited, happy, and proud? Confident, grounded, and grateful?

Congrats! They feel similar vibes for you! This is in alignment and will feel like what we dreamed business could be like. I like to try to be the kind of client I also want to have.

Think of a customer situation that was sticky or tricky. We're not going to villainize them—this is for you to understand so you can better attract and serve the people you are uniquely suited to help. Back to that sticky customer situation. What were you feeling? Dread, not-enough-ness, or avoidance? Frustration, judgment, or resentment?

If you go back to the beginning of the relationship with them, what could have been off? Sometimes, it's that you ignored a red flag or two, not honoring your intuition. Sometimes, it is that you wanted it to be a good fit so much that you were willing to bend your boundaries and maybe skipped a step in your process.

Sometimes, you wanted them to be comfy, so you people-pleased your way into a situation that was out of alignment, and now *you're* uncomfortable. Maybe they came in at a time when you felt as if you had to say yes to any business you could get because you didn't like what your bank app said.

> **We are all learning. None of us have ever been here before.**

Maybe you were following a marketing guru's scarcity tactics and drew in customers who were hooked by the scarcity-inducing words, and now it's all feeling off. Please don't beat yourself up for any of it. We are all learning. None of us have ever been here before, as my friend Wendy so compassionately says when I want to shame myself for a lesson.

We can take solace in knowing that when we are "cooking with gas" and draw in the best customer experiences, it will be long-lasting, and no one can take that ripple away. And you can take heart in knowing that when you realize a customer isn't the best fit for you, they get to find alignment elsewhere, and you now have more helpful intel for your next steps. That's invaluable.

The other bonus is that when we energetically release—albeit uncomfortable, at times—clients who are better served elsewhere, we make room for new, ideal clients to come in, and that is a beautiful exercise in trusting your business.

> **Let's get curious through the squirm. It will be worth it.**

There's a practical way to have your finger on the pulse of your alignment. You can always check your current results and experience. If you have a business full of great customers, keep on truckin'. You're on a roll. If you feel frustrated all the time, it's just another way your business is here to help you heal. Let's get curious through the squirm. It will be worth it.

I'm going to say something hard here. It might be activating for you. I need to give you a heads-up that you can come back to this or skip it if you're not ready to dig deep and use this as a tool for your growth, not a weapon to make yourself wrong. Because this applies to everyone I've ever met. Me too!

I am constantly walking my brain back home to more helpful options.

Ok . . . ready?

This beautiful business of yours is always showing you what you believe. Believe that your product and service are amazing, totally worth the investment, your customers and clients get incredible results and love to tell their friends—and you will likely see customers and clients raving and getting awesome results.

And you can probably already predict the other side of the coin.

> **This beautiful business of yours is always showing you what you believe.**

When we face clients and customers who are not ideal for us and don't see the value in what we provide, we have to ask ourselves some important leadership questions and answer with raw truth.

Am I delivering on my promises?

Have I honored my side of the agreement? (Only our stuff, not their part.)

Have I been out of belief with my offer or product?

Where am I not valuing what I do?

If you honestly deliver on your part of the agreement and show up in your integrity, you can sleep well at night. Rest easy. It's not always you.

What this does not mean:

Making it your fault if your customer or client does not do their part.

I had a client who started getting bad reviews and terrible comments about her product. This was way out of the norm for the successful company. They realized that what was happening was their product was the target of cheap knock-offs, and the people complaining had bought from a pretty obvious fake site.

This was not the fault of the business owner. Her team got busy educating customers on how to buy the real product and, thankfully, did not shame themselves for customer mistakes. That is THEIR stuff. In fact, those folks were never actually customers—they just thought they were.

I just talked to a friend this morning who found out that some of her clients were complaining about her price going up. NOT HER STUFF. She could easily internalize it and make herself wrong for raising prices. We can always people-please ourselves right into the red and suffer financially. Their thoughts about pricing are theirs to own, not yours.

One of my coaches always talks about how there is NO right price. People complain about free things too! And while it is not her stuff, it still offers a helpful mirror. Remember, when we squirm, it's a chance to get curious and learn. What does she believe about her new prices? These folks are actors in her play. What is this showing her?

When you are faced with the discernment of what is yours and what is theirs, you can ask yourself: What is my motivation for offering my service or product at this higher price? Most often, it's because it will be more sustainable. That's always in the best interest of our customers. Why? Because if we are exhausted and broke, there's no more service or product for the people we're here to help.

I haven't met a businesswoman who's out to just gouge. That is totally projection from the people who have their own money stuff to look at. Are there high investment levels for some businesses? Yes. Is that a problem? No. Our judgment about it is.

If your motives are to create a more sustainable business, you can safely move into checking out what kind of projection that person(s) may be experiencing. I would get curious about price complaints, with love. Why on earth would a woman want another woman to not be resourced? We need more loving, resourced, empowered women on the planet. Anyone who isn't ready for that idea is being called up to their own healing too.

That is not your issue. Unless it is?

It's possible, because we are all humans living a very human experience, that you might be having your own price judgment. So here come the people judging your prices. Makes sense, right? Remember, this is all coming up to help us heal. Actors in our play.

This is not the end of the world, but I can say with certainty (and love!) that your abundance is likely being slowed way down if you are judging prices. I think of it like a garden hose. When there is a kink in the hose (something that wants to be looked at and loved on—like price judgment), the water just can't flow. Think of the hair stylist who wants to make more money so she can spend less time on her feet also sitting in *her* stylist's chair judging the prices. This is a kink in the abundance hose.

If you have been complaining about another business owner's pricing, I'm going to guess this is part of your healing process. Where do you judge your own prices? We've got to notice and love ourselves through this kind of thought. Because if you're thinking it, so are your clients.

Bottom line: we pay for what we value.

Now, the prudent money beliefs might be already yelling, "But, Sarah! I care about my budget, and I can't just willy nilly throw wads of cash at other businesses all the time just so I can make money in *my* business!" Let's just give that scared part of you a hug. This is not a tit-for-tat scenario. You don't automatically get paid $5,000 because you bought something for $5,000. You don't have to ever give away your spending sovereignty.

Bottom line: we pay for what we value. What we value will be unique to us. Earlier in the book, I mentioned that powerful thought about our values showing us our boundaries. If you do not value something, please don't pay for it. Let's call that price discernment. That comes from inside you—what you value and are willing to exchange money for in order to receive it. Can you feel the difference when you think of discernment versus judgment?

Price judgment comes from a wound.

Price judgment comes from a wound. A belief about what someone should or should not be able to ask for in exchange for their product or service can hamper your wealth building, so I invite you to get curious. You can ask yourself the powerful question I learned from Brené Brown: "What story am I making up?"[6]

That story holds some gold. What you make someone's price mean, or what you make it mean when someone does or does not purchase from you or invest with you, is solid gold intel when it comes to your growth. But when you see it for what it is, you can alchemize it.

That story likely goes back to a time when you didn't feel safe or didn't have a choice. Maybe you were struggling to get by. Maybe you saw people make money and then make poor choices with it or treat people badly, and your brain made the association that money equals greed or evil. We've got unlimited cultural examples of the mean rich lady or the mean powerful lady in movies, so even if you didn't grow up hearing successful humans being cut down by gossip or whispers, you had plenty of places to subconsciously pick up money stories.

The great news is this is not a pass/fail situation. You get to practice for the rest of your life. As long as you are operating a business, you will charge a price and receive payment for it. You are probably practicing right now.

How do you want to think about your prices moving forward?

Perfection is not required; this will always be a process of receiving what we want and recalibrating when we don't. We truly do want the best for people, and if the best thing for them isn't doing business with us right now, releasing them with love is healing for you both. We are making room for more joy!

Let me introduce you to a concept I call a "power thought." It is a proactive way to choose how you want to think about a squirmy situation. It calls you forward to the results you want to create. As we heal and grow, we will run into situations where a client leaves or rejects our price. We can end up in reactive mode, which only adds suffering, or we can create a power thought that draws in more of what we do desire.

> Example: A reactive thought about a client who doesn't like your price could be, "My prices are too expensive."
>
> A power thought about the same exact situation could be, "Aligned, resourced, ready buyers are finding me right now."

Your turn.

A helpful power thought when it comes to my clients:

A power thought when it comes to my price:

A power thought about the value of the results I provide:

Our Team Members

Just as our clients are here to help us heal, so are the team members we bring into our business. If I had a dollar for every minute I coached an incredible business owner on a team member situation that was exhausting her, I could retire tomorrow.

More actors in our play. This time, though, we add in the bonus (sarcasm) of paying them to kick up frustration, disappointment, fear, and resentment. If one of our loved ones triggers us, we don't have to then turn around and write them a paycheck.

Yikes.

Yet it happens day in and day out. Most of my clients are golden-hearted givers. I've started saying over-givers because by the time they come to me, they've poured out of an empty pitcher for one too many pay periods.

I have had the honor of healing my stuff thanks to many team members in my entrepreneurial experience. Each human on my team inspired me to evolve—some through winning, teamwork, and feel-good times, and some through disappointing and downright shocking scenarios.

For the most part, I was blessed to find employees who gave it their all. It's how we built a beautiful magazine and scaled it to seven times its reach and revenue. It's how we built an award-winning marketing agency that helped so many companies and nonprofits across the globe. It's how I created a company that loves me back now. Each team member's fingerprint is on my history book of business, and I love them for that.

> **Each "mistake" I made was part of my play, and they were the actors.**

And each team member who didn't help me win in obvious ways still helped me win. Each time I people-pleased my way into hardship for myself, I learned how it felt to be out of alignment. The more dramatic the misalignment, the more healing I had to face for myself. I learned how to build more courage for the next conversation I'd need to have. I learned how to lead with love, even when that meant leading them out the glass front doors, ending our relationship.

Each "mistake" I made was part of my play, and they were the actors. It was easy to feel victimized and taken for granted when I saw some of the situations unfolding. Now I'm so grateful to have gone through those challenges because they help me navigate similar scenarios with my coaching clients so they can learn from me and avoid years of unnecessary suffering.

I'll never forget one of my clients coming in hot to a session, ready to talk about her administrative assistant, who was consuming all of my client's bandwidth—and she didn't have any extra to waste. This team member was a drain on morale and was no longer a match for where my client wanted to take her company. There were plenty of valid reasons to end this person's employment. But there were lots of guilt-based reasons to keep hanging on. So, she did.

My client was caretaking to the point of resentment. Her big heart had long been bled dry, and she was giving from fear at this point. This team member had been going through things at home, and my client wanted to be there for her. Years passed, and nothing changed with the employee's home life, and the work performance continued to slide. My client had nothing but loyalty left to go on. Because this person was there with her in the beginning, she felt beholden.

> What we don't realize is that we could end up *blocking the blessing* for our team members when we hold on out of guilt.

What we don't realize is that we could end up *blocking the blessing* for our team members when we hold on out of guilt.

That one concept helped me overcome the strong pull of it. What if, by hanging on, we do them a disservice?

No one wants to be a drain on morale. Maybe a job change would be the fresh air they need.

No one wants to frustrate their boss. It isn't truly caring for them if you look at them and want to scream every day. Your high-performing team members suffer too.

What message does guilt-driven tolerance send to the folks who give it their all? What does it do for your energy? How many hours of your day do you spend overthinking it or worrying about it? What would those hours total if you billed for them? (She had a billable rate, by-the-hour business, and it added up to tens of thousands of dollars' worth of her time and energy.)

My client got coached up, made her painful decision, and got her documentation ready (always follow HR protocol). She had the tough conversation. She grew more confident in her leadership with that conversation. It was sad for her, but she was clear it was over.

By the next time we coached, she was a lighter, happier version of herself. She said that the whole office became uplifted and more productive. That team member was now free to focus on her family (not bypassing the painful reality that it is hard to lose a job). This was a huge turning point in my client's business. She went on to scale rapidly in the coming years. She had bandwidth again to pursue her biggest goals.

If you were to summarize the best leadership courses, books, and concepts, they all boil down to this: If the people on your team are not helping you get closer to your goals, it's time to evaluate. If they have the information, safety, and tools they need to do their jobs, and they are not, it's time for your business to help you heal a leadership wound.

> **If the people on your team are not helping you get closer to your goals, it's time to evaluate.**

One of the best ways to know if you're being called up to leadership is by watching how you act around this team member. I'll tell on myself here with the hopes it will make you smirk every time you find yourself doing something similar.

I always knew I was being called up to lead when I would take extra measures to avoid a certain team member. In 2018, we bought an office building with a hallway that would circle the whole building. You could go left or right and still access all the offices. I did not have to walk by certain offices if I didn't want to.

One of my "tells" that I needed to take a serious look at my leadership was that I started avoiding walking by a certain team member's office. I would make it a point to go around it so I wouldn't have to see her. This was supposed to be the human to whom I delegated everything on my to-do list to, but I didn't want to deal with the problems that kept popping up with her.

I continued to avoid her office, as if it was going to get better if I just ignored it. The people pleaser in me did NOT want to have what Gay Hendricks in *The Big Leap* book calls the "sweaty ten-minute conversation that you don't want to have."[7] I wanted to keep my status as "nice boss."

Well, it got so bad that other people in our organization were coming to me with issues too. One day, my friend, who was also our cleaning helper at the office, staged her own intervention with me and the employee about her concerns. It's slightly humorous to look back on now, seeing how ridiculous it was for me to avoid a human I was paying to help me. Cringe. Huge kudos to my friend who stopped what she was doing during her cleaning gig to be a courageous leader when I wasn't stepping up. She said what needed to be said. It gave me enough of a push to address the other ongoing issues.

I did end up needing to eventually release this team member. I'll never forget the glare I got as she walked out the door. It was the first time a firing didn't end with mutual well-wishes or even a hug. This one was a little scary, but it did bring us both back into alignment. How do I know it helped her align? She wrote a letter about a year later thanking me because it was what she needed. She got on a different growth path and totally kicks butt in her own business now.

Some show us how we shine, and others will help us polish up our skills.

She was an actor in my play. So was my cleaning helper friend. Every team member is. Some show us how we shine, and others will help us polish up our skills. I invite you to consider where someone on your team is creating an opportunity for growth.

You can ask yourself these questions:

What would help me show up in my values better?

What boundaries are being crossed?

Where am I feeling resentful or taken for granted?

What am I nervous about?

What is my next right step?

What part of my leadership is being asked to step up right now?

Our Relationships

The darkest times in my marriage came while being business partners. It wasn't because we'd never worked together. We had a decade of side-by-side daily co-working. But our businesses brought to light every pain point.

My husband and I have been married nearly twenty years now, and we worked together for twenty-two years straight. Every day. We met at the CBS station in Springfield, Missouri, where we were both reporters and anchors. Destiny stepped in, we fell in love, got married, and we moved to Wisconsin, where we would both work for the NBC station until we left news for entrepreneurship.

In dog years (which I totally think qualifies for math on spouses who work together), that would be more than a century. When viewers asked, "How do you do it?" I would joke, saying, "We don't know any better because this is how it's always been!"

Fast forward into the stresses of owning and growing two companies together, and let's just light the match and throw it on the dry tinder of any wobbly issues in your marriage.

Poof—instant burns.

I coach clients all the time who have someone in their life—spouse, parent, business partner—who kicks up every painful pattern for them too. So, as I write this book, I am here to share the most important pieces I've learned. Our businesses absolutely kick up our relationship issues. (Insert any close relationship that seems to trigger as you grow your business; this does not have to be your spouse.) Gratefully, I am on the other side of so much healing that our marriage is better today than it ever has been. I wasn't so sure a few years back.

> **Our businesses absolutely kick up our relationship issues.**

We are opposites in many ways (big surprise—I imagine your story is similar), which used to balance us out. We'd be talking about problems, and one of us would be chill while the other freaked out. It worked for many years. As our marketing agency grew, so did the pressure. The payroll, the overhead, and the client demands put us in a vice grip of constant stress.

Pretty soon, it was coming out sideways. Our mindsets were getting further and further apart from a helpful consensus. The way we wanted to lead was night-and-day opposite. The team noticed. I tried to people-please everyone, including him, but we were beginning to become adversaries in broad daylight. Our team needed united leadership, and we didn't have it.

It caused a lot of pain. But it was happening *for* us. At the time, it was a lot of tearful nights where my wounds were begging him to see my side of things. I might as well have been shouting into the abyss. He couldn't hear me because his thoughts and fears were too loud. The stories we were both making up about the challenges we faced were making us enemies.

This rough patch lasted a long time. Scaling our company meant more team members and more money circulating. More unhelpful fear surfaced, and no matter how much cash rolled in, or how many lunches we took away from the office, the arguments and disagreements kept happening.

We existed like this for years. It wasn't all bad, not by a long shot. We had a lot of fun too. But that's not the point of this chapter. Thankfully, our kids kept us focused on what we did agree on at home. There was no time to do anything other than be parents there, but the tension usually followed us through the front door of our home.

As fate would have it, we each started an additional business during this stressful time. (Because, why not, right?) A business that didn't include the other spouse. His was commercial real estate, and mine was The Juicy Good Life. This gave us something new to focus on but would expose more of a rift as time went on. I would still be the point person at our agency, leaning on our amazing project manager to ensure clients were happy. The awards for achievement and philanthropy flooded in for the agency and for me personally, but what I started to notice was that while others cheered, my husband would literally glare at me as I moved about the office on those award luncheon days.

It was truly one of the hardest things for a woman who naturally cheerleads others to feel so unsupported by her life and business partner. The cheers of others were drowned out by his visible resentment. This pattern had surfaced so many times in my personal life that it had become my two-by-four. I had another close person in my life who had a habit of making a scene on big days for me. My wedding, ribbon cuttings, a big Woman of Achievement award night. It was an eerily similar vibe. My wound was raw. He didn't have to make a scene for it to feel like the same salt being poured into a deep cut from my past. He just had to look at me sideways and I was triggered.

> **What was it trying to show me? Stop going to the hardware store for milk.**

What was it trying to show me? Stop going to the hardware store for milk. See what needs were not being met and get to meeting them myself. Take really good care of myself and follow my heart. Set boundaries and hold them.

What did it want me to heal? I wanted others to act like I would. I tried to control the situation by trying to make them happy "enough" so they would support me. I expected my support to be reciprocated. I also fell into old reactions that I learned from my parents. That led to me yelling and using volume and pleading to try to get the other person to see my "side."

It reinforced the importance of having a true support system made up of people who are doing their inner healing so they can help you sort through what's yours and what's not yours. To witness your feelings and gently encourage you to set boundaries. Thank goodness for friends who will love you and listen every time you are in the same patterns. I leaned on my bestie so much during this time. It helps that she is a marriage and family therapist by trade, and she fully understands who I am. (Thank you, Rachelle.)

It had to get painful enough so I would make a decision to shift. To decide I was not going to live like that anymore. I got a ton of therapy, got coached all the time, and doubled down on my healing classes and practices. I chose to honor my integrity, heal my own crap, and follow my intuition.

I was not perfect but was committed to keeping my side of the street clean. My husband is really good at setting boundaries for how we show up in arguments, and it was time for me to heal my pattern of fighting as a means to be heard. I worked on it. I said the hard things and named it when his actions hurt. I got my own support instead from my friends when I was tempted to head to that hardware store for milk (looking to him for cheerleading). I listened more to his perspective. His fear was that we were no longer a team. That makes sense because I had changed so much, I wasn't the same team member anymore.

The key learning for me included what codependency actually is, and I started learning Alcoholics Anonymous and

Al-Anon concepts since my family tree was full of alcoholism. I didn't realize how it affects every aspect of life when you're growing up in the behaviors and trauma responses of that trickle-down effect on your entire ecosystem.

I owned what was mine to own—imperfectly choosing to have my own back and let my loved ones choose their paths and be in the consequences of their behavior. I kept crying and crying every time it hurt or I fell into old patterns that disempowered me. I was no longer just numbing my wounds. I was feeling the big feelings I didn't have access to before. I was in the painful squirm of facing all of the hurt, old and new.

Over time, the more I healed *me*, the more my husband could meet me where I was at. I could actually be open to what he had to share. My healing made room for new realizations. The less I locked down in frustration and resentment, the freer I felt to focus on building my Juicy Good Life.

I did enough healing work on myself that I got to a point where I was willing to walk away from the old dynamics to save my sanity. My business did that for me. Everything I helped my coaching clients get—peace, ease, joy—I chose that for me too.

It was time to set down the old ways. From the outside, I worried it was going to look like I was blowing up my life. But I was just sunsetting what was ready to go.

I decided I would retire from our marketing agency. My husband's nervous system was not ready to hear that. The day I shared that decision with him and asked him how he would like to proceed (there were several options; I was just not going to be one of them anymore), I heard all of my silent fears come out of his mouth. It was rough. I feared not only the agency days would be over but that our marriage wouldn't survive the phaseout either. As I reflected on this with him recently (we're nearly three years past this dark time), he doesn't remember it being as dramatic as I do. It was never about him. All of this painful squirm was for me to choose to reduce my own suffering and amplify my own joy. We can only ever control ourselves. We can invite the people we love to join us, but in the end, it's all happening to help us evolve.

> We can only ever control ourselves. We can invite the people we love to join us, but in the end, it's all happening to help us evolve.

He was the actor in my play big-time. It called me up to courage in every way possible. I was living in the results of my decision to sunset our agency. Now I had to figure out how to pay for the massive overhead that still existed from that big machine we built while scaling my coaching company so it could sustain us all.

I decided I would hold the vision of the life I believed we could have. I held that vision through an entire year of tearfully confronting my scarcity and his loud doubts about my coaching company's ability to maintain our life the way we wanted. It was wobbly and awful, and I wouldn't wish it on anyone, but I totally see how it shaped me for my next phase of growth.

That was as painful as it is poetic now as I write it. Instead of begging or forcing my husband to get on board with the future I wanted for us, I started to craft it for myself, and that made room for him to meet me in a new version of our marriage. I am super clear that I won't tolerate bad behavior, and I also own my part fully. I had to unlearn my overcontrol tactics. They were built from my wounds in childhood. The way I could maneuver to get what I needed to feel safe. The way I kept score instead of asking for what I needed. He married a people pleaser who would bend over backward for anyone. He married the fixer of the emotions. The orchestrator of the comfort. I wasn't that person anymore.

So, he had to get to know this new version of me.

Heck, so did I.

But by a full miracle, it turns out that when you heal, you are not healed alone.[8] It doesn't mean I did all the heavy lifting for us; I just made room for something new to come in. My business led the way. It showed me everything I needed to heal the old wounds that wanted to take down my marriage at the time.

We both had to be fully awake to our decision to be in a healthy, happy partnership. We had to learn how to communicate differently. We had to learn how to advocate for ourselves and our needs so we could come to the marriage more whole and grounded. We had to learn how to not let scarcity ruin our day. And, most obviously, we had to learn not to be that side-by-side team at work. We no longer run a company together. That era was complete. That was the hardest part, according to my husband. To reimagine what teamwork would be moving forward after so many years of being shoulder-to-shoulder in the daily grind.

> When you heal, you are not healed alone.

We have new gratitude for our dark days. He has new perspective after being out from under the daily stress, and we continue to heal from it. Not gonna lie—there are some subjects that are still too tender around our old company that we just can't go there yet. I am compassionate for both of our old selves. I see how my people-pleasing pattern with our team made him the enemy. I can now have gratitude for the parts of him that helped me grow.

I am also wide awake to what's not mine to own in our marriage. And because we were both willing to look at our wounds and work through them via some serious and painful squirming, I am deeply happy to report that when something good happens for me, I get a love note now.

Just the other day, I had a painful moment, and he just looked me in the eye, witnessing my pain, and gave me the longest, most supportive embrace I have ever felt from him. I'm bawling just thinking about it. This is a miracle. A MIRACLE. He is now able to be there for me and our kids in ways I could only dream about before. It is a divine gift. I thank our businesses for kicking up all our wounds so they could be held with love as we healed them. Our happier marriage is a direct result of the painful squirm our business brought up.

We are only able to control our choices, but the ripple is real. I see it all the time. A business owner decides to start owning what's hers to heal, learning what wounds are really at play, deciding to prioritize her mental well-being; what's not meant for her falls away, and what *is* meant for her shifts in some way.

Is it perfect? No.

Are you required to shoulder everything? No.

Should you put up with abuse? Never.

If you want out, you get to get out. Always.

This relationship story is not your story.

This relationship story is not your story. You don't have to stay and suffer if that is not right for you. I have had to choose no contact to protect my peace with another loved one who is simply not safe for me. I'm doing my healing, but not in tandem with them. I've experienced multiple different endings to relationships that were no longer healthy for me, and my wish for you is to honor your needs every step of the way.

If you believe it is safe and healthy for you to heal in a relationship and you want to stay in the one you're thinking of as you read this chapter, begin by getting curious about what's up for review.

Here's what can help as you sort through the relationship patterns that show up:

What is my most desired outcome with this person?

Do I believe we are capable and resourced (emotionally and mentally) to reach that outcome?

If not, what would have to happen? Is that in my control?

What am I available for, and what am I not available for?

What is my personal plan if boundaries are not honored?

If my pain had a voice here, what would it want me to know?

What are my values, or where do I need boundaries so I can honor them?

Do I know the other person's values, and how is that factoring into our dynamic?

What are our roles? Are we staying in our lanes?

What decision-making power do I have or do I want?

What decision does my most healed self need to make?

What stories am I telling myself about this?

What bad behaviors am I witnessing from them?

Where do I need to own my part in our dynamics?

What healing and support would be most helpful for me right now?

Who are the trusted supporters I can reach out to?

What choices do I want to make for my most empowered future?

Braving Your Wounds

Naming the Wounds

What did you think you'd need when you started your business? A logo? Website? Social media presence? Business cards? Accounting software? All of that, for sure.

Maybe you got jazzed about going to the office supply store. Maybe it was getting that new desk and chair and cute lamp that looked so amazing in your own workspace.

I love all of this too. I fully geek out on all the goodies that kick off our company. I would argue that it's the nesting that helps us bond with our business. It's important. We have to have some fun, or what are we even doing here?

But all the branding bliss comes with a quick realization that we are about to meet every wound we've ever had in a new way. When I say wound, I'm describing an old hurt that perhaps you formed some beliefs around. Perhaps it was a phrase or directive you heard growing up from a well-meaning loved one, and it backfires or haunts you in your business.

When we are out of alignment or are tender and depleted, these wounds will want to be our CEO, calling the shots subconsciously if we are asleep to them. But good news; you're reading this book, and I can be that friend on the front porch of business with you, letting you in on what might be happening when you're in the squirm.

> **These wounds will want to be our CEO, calling the shots subconsciously.**

As with every single concept I bring, please just take what resonates and leave the rest. There may be concepts that don't apply to you. Maybe they will make sense in another season—or never. That's okay. The biggest gift you can give yourself is to stay open to what could help you love yourself more when you are meeting a wound or two along the way.

I don't have the exhaustive list because wounds are so varied. Yours will be unique to you. I've done my best to collect some universal wounds and patterns that I see showing up and creating challenges for the women I help the most. We're going to look at how you'll meet money wounds, people-pleasing patterns, visibility fears, perfectionism, and overall cultural conditioning that holds us back from being our true self.

Your business is divinely sent to help you heal the wounds that hold you back from feeling rooted in the freedom of being yourself.

> Your business is divinely sent to help you heal the wounds that hold you back from feeling rooted in the freedom of being yourself.

On the other side of the squirm is everything you want and more. It's so worth it.

They Change Outfits

One of the most helpful ways to know what your business can help you heal is to look out for your patterns. Patterns are the challenges, situations, or feelings that keep coming up for you. They come up again and again because they want to be shifted. They want to be loved on. They want to be healed.

I love the idea I read about once. I wish I could remember the source, but it talked about our problems changing outfits. Same problem, new twist. One day, it shows up in how we deal with our money; the next day, it could "change outfits" and show up in a fight we have with a spouse. When we get to the actual issue, not just the topic, the underlying wound is the same, but the way it shows up is just different enough to keep us thinking it's a new problem.

It might come in the form of a to-do list that feels overwhelming. It might show up in your health or in your bank account. It might show up in your parenting or in your networking. None of us get through business growth without coming face-to-face with our patterns. Remember, this beautiful business was divinely sent so you could have a catalyst for healing what doesn't work so you can get to what does.

> **None of us get through business growth without coming face-to-face with our patterns.**

Many of my clients work with me long enough so I can help them find the pattern's root cause: I call it the core wound. We can have several wounds, but often, they will boil down to one big hurt from the past. You have probably heard of the "mother wound" (and yes, our core wound may boil down to caregiver trauma) or something similar, but as we get to know ourselves, we'll find something unique to us.[9] Many of my clients will have a belief that formed for good reason, as a result of a trauma, but it will continue to show up in business and try to take the wheel if we don't lovingly explore it with the proper channels of support.

Mine sounds like, "You're doing it wrong." The flip side of it is, "You gotta get it right." It's the same wound. Do it right, or I'm not safe. In my childhood, high expectations were the norm. Corporal punishment (zero out of ten stars, do not recommend spankings) was the answer for my parents to ensure we did things right. Makes sense why I'm still wanting to get stuff right in my forties. It took me this long to connect the dots on my core wound. I just labeled it as being an achiever and didn't think much more about it.

I've been on a healing path, as in weekly, deep trauma healing, for nearly a decade, and this only became really clear to me this year. It's really freaking painful to realize where it came from (especially as I see my kids at the ages I was experiencing so much turmoil), so I have help from my coaches, a therapist using Eye Movement Desensitization and Reprocessing (EMDR), and from my spiritual teacher in a weekly healing class where we do all kinds of work with different modalities like Emotional Freedom Technique (EFT), working with our Human Design, and most recently Neuro Emotional Technique (NET). These have been blessings to me, and you will find what works for you.

My "you gotta get it right" wound shows up everywhere. For sure, while writing this book.

Absolutely shows up with my money management and big time with my budding advocacy in the world. My parenting? Yep. Marriage? You bet. I'd be hard-pressed to find an area of life where the "you gotta get it right" vibe isn't at play. But now I can see it and love myself through the squirm of choosing my truth.

The truth is, I don't have to get it right. I'm not doing it wrong. I'm learning; I'm in pursuit of being my most healed, loving, authentic self. There is no wrong way to be me. There is no wrong way to be you. There is no right way to do this life. All of the harsh rules I lived by are actually made up to keep me hustling for those gold stars I don't even need anymore. I'm so grateful each of my businesses were conduits for me to uncover new parts of me. If it wasn't for my desire and need to grow my companies, there is no way I'd show up as dedicated to take a look at my "stuff" as I have been.

> **There is no wrong way to be me.**
> **There is no wrong way to be you.**

It might take years for you to find your patterns and your patterns' root causes. My hope is that by reading this book, you will have new tools to see what might want healing for you.

The reason it can take a while is that whole new outfit thing. We could argue that many of the outfits are a shade of camouflage.

Most of us come with problems like, "I'm not selling," or "I'm not charging enough," or "I'm doing all the work," but there is a pattern dressed up as an annoying or frustrating challenge.

Once you see it and understand it, you have the key to more peace and compassion in your life. You begin to move through your stressors with so much more ease and speed than in the past.

I just heard from a client before I sat down to write this chapter. She thanked me for this work we do together because she just had a situation that she said would have taken her out for weeks, and she didn't react like she used to because she has new tools to trust herself more and not take on the projections of others.

Another client realized her rumination about her to-do list was deeply rooted in her core wound of not feeling worthy. This one even surprised me as I coached her. To-do list stress is so common, so normal among female business owners that when she got to that awareness in a private session, we were both in awe. She cracked the code on so much of her suffering. Now that she has this awareness, she's loving herself through it and noticing so much faster when it changes outfits and shows up in other places in her life—like in her physical health and her finances.

Core wounds can sound like this:

> I'm not enough.
> I'm not safe.
> I'm not worthy.
> I'm alone.

The outfits they can change into sound like this:

> I have to do it myself.
> I need more money.
> The other shoe is going to drop.
> No one understands me.
> I have to do it right.
> What if I fail?
> I have to push through.
> I'm overwhelmed.
> I'm stuck.
> I don't know what to do.
> It's taking too long.

The list is endless, but just see what's rising for you. When we're in a nervous system activation from something that triggered our wound, we don't have access to the 30,000-foot view that can help us see what's actually going on. This is why coaching is so powerful. It's so much easier to see what's truly happening when you have someone to weed through it with you.

As you read on, I'll be covering some of the biggest challenges I see in female business owners. See what seems to speak to your heart. Bring along your knowing that you are not wrong and bad (aka shame) if you see multiple patterns that resonate. Let yourself remember that the pattern(s) is something that wants to be loved on more. Be gentle with yourself.

Be gentle with yourself.

This is knowledge that can make life a lot less rough on you. When we know our patterns, we shine a light on them. Shame cannot exist in the light of compassion. We are choosing to bring the light of compassion with every new aha.

Let's light the candle of compassion as we go.

Generational Trauma

Some of your wounds may be the result of generational trauma. Your parents, grandparents, and great-grandparents (and truly all of their parents going way back in your lineage) went through traumatic things, and if no one interrupts those patterns and heals them, you may be dealing with lingering ramifications of things your ancestors experienced.

Women who are inspired to start a business want to make the world a better place. It might start with making the world better for yourself. For me, it was my kiddos first; then I realized how entrepreneurship healed so much of my generational trauma.

Cycle-breaking is no joke, but I can't imagine a better scenario than us being able to cope better so our next generation doesn't have to heal from the same things. They will have their own stuff to navigate, but I'm grateful my children won't equate having a career with needing to sacrifice health, happiness, and well-being. That cycle has been broken.

> Women who are inspired to start a business want to make the world a better place. It might start with making the world better for yourself.

When we are healing our generational trauma, we can focus a lot on the frustration and hurt, but as we face the truth of the hardships, we can find compassion in it all. Healing generational trauma doesn't have to feel dishonoring to our family, but rather a conscious choice to bring the best of the family forward instead of unconsciously recreating that pain over and over. I learned a ton from my parents. I still use the people skills and ingenuity they taught me to this day.

As we move through the different ways our wounds show up for healing, you will likely see how they affected people in your family tree. Things we saw the adults in our lives do to cope (they probably still do) will make more sense. The way they dealt (or didn't) with the hardships and triggers will be easier to understand as you understand yours.

Unhealed trauma runs the world in many ways. Let's decide that we are going to let the more healed versions of ourselves run our businesses and better our lives.

People-Pleasing

Several years ago, I was getting coached on something I felt nervous about with a client. After my coaching session, I was journaling about my feelings, and the lightbulb kicked on. What I realized was that I was trying to fix something for them, and it was leading to over-giving, over-caretaking, and I wasn't seeing her want it for herself as much as I wanted it for her.

My journaling revealed the thought: "If you're not ok, I'm not ok."

Oh, DANG.

This situation where I wanted the result more than the client did was kicking up all my people-pleaser stuff. It wanted to be healed. I got coached on it. I was reminded that only I can create the feeling of safety my nervous system wanted.

But before I saw the wound for what it was (a need for safety), I was really busy giving everything I could to help this client see certain results. I wasn't leaving room for them to have their aha because I feared it would come at a painful price. I was over-caretaking.

Thankfully, I cleaned up my side of the street and got my own buns coached on where I was stepping out of coach mode and into people-pleaser mode. I saw my patterns of wanting results more than the people in my life did. Here it was again. Turns out, it changed outfits enough times that it was my turn to look at how I created that dynamic.

We need compassion for where this wound likely developed. We were probably young and found a way to meet our needs by making life easier for those around us. We were likely rewarded for being such a good helper.

We can LOVE being a helper and let that come forth from a place of healthy giving. When it swings into over-giving is when we need to tend to our wound.

My brain had been well-trained to be the fixer. I cannot remember a time I wasn't the peacekeeper and good little helper. I learned along the line to keep everyone happy so my system could feel more at ease, and I could get the attagirls I became so used to. The other option was not safe. Conflict, unhappiness, and turmoil in others would become my problem as a child and all through my life. I served as a referee and fixer for decades. It worked for me. Until it didn't.

It turns out that in business, if your people pleaser runs the show long enough, you will end up exhausted, broke, and resentful of it all. There are just too many humans you'd have to caretake and not enough of you to go around. If we keep it really basic, our people-pleasing shows up so that we don't have to feel the squirm. It's a temporary relief that, unfortunately, ends up leading to potential resentment in the long run.

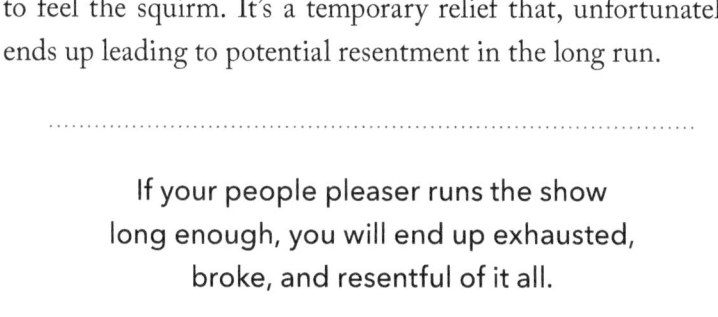

If your people pleaser runs the show long enough, you will end up exhausted, broke, and resentful of it all.

We discount our services without being asked just so we don't have to feel the squirm of seeing someone else decide if they agree with our price. We throw in bonuses and give away time so our clients feel extra cared for so they stay happy and our business stays safe from complaints. We make payment plans when we really want payment in full, up front. But our squirm with having to say no is more uncomfortable at the time than ignoring our business boundaries. We avoid the squirm, but that's what comes back to bite us later.

When we can get to the root of what this part of you needs—coaching, EMDR, and parts work was very helpful for me with a therapist, an Internal Family Systems (IFS) professional—you become more grounded and confident and create more safety inside yourself. Pretty soon, with practice, you don't flinch when it comes time to hold steady in a business boundary.

This can save tons of your energy, and that energy can be freed up to build your business with humans you don't have to fix it for all the time. You become a magnet to people who will do their own work when you no longer bend over backward to do it for them. Your more grounded self doesn't draw in all the old actors in your play because you don't need as much practice.

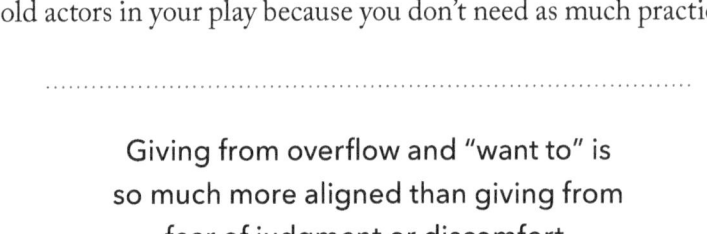

> Giving from overflow and "want to" is so much more aligned than giving from fear of judgment or discomfort.

Then you start to realize that giving from overflow and "want to" is so much more aligned than giving from fear of judgment or discomfort. We can give that helper in us, who we love so much, a new job. Give when it is FUN to give! Give from joy! Give from wanting to reward your customers. It's a whole new vibe.

And P.S. It will make you more money in the long run when you do.

I'll never forget two of my clients who started working with me. Both had discounts built into their business. This offering was just a given; they hadn't thought about it much. When we dug in, we found out that, for the most part, it was just a way to feel safer in their business. We also discovered that this accidental people-pleasing added up to more than $30,000! This is what my inner business strategist calls a profit leak.

One of these clients had carried over this discount mindset from the franchise she was working with. They had a "butts in seats" mentality and believed discounts were the way to get people to sign up. My client knew that the true draw to her business was the fun and memories they made there. But she kept offering discounted sessions. She realized in coaching that what it actually did was train people to wait for a coupon.

When I asked her about sticking with the full-price session, her fear revealed a people-pleaser moment. She was worried people would complain. I asked her if her ideal clients would complain, and she said no. Turns out, the complainers would complain! She actually dreaded going to sessions with the folks who would be the loudest about the coupon changes. They not only came in at a lower price, but they were higher maintenance! We laughed, and she made a new business boundary that day.

In a few short weeks, her customer base was happily used to paying full price, and they were having a great time. She was enjoying her business more, putting thousands more in her pocket while not adding any work. She did way less emotional labor (no longer tending to coupon complaints) and much less admin (no longer tracking coupons). She was enjoying showing up for happy customers, who couldn't wait to pay her full price. When she wanted to offer a coupon, she did it as a treat to her loyal customers, and they were surprised and delighted.

So. Juicy.

We call this a win, win, win.

I don't want to sugarcoat it; it might be squirmy as heck. Especially the first several times you say no to over-giving and fixing it. But like my client found out, it's worth the squirm. She transformed her happiness and her profits with one empowered decision. And as my friend and fellow coach Suzanne Culberg says, "When you stop people-pleasing, some people will not be pleased."[10]

You have to love your reasons enough to have your own back during the squirm. It's where I spend most of my energy with clients as their business coach. I'm with them in the squirm, and we celebrate when they make confident moves to the other side of the squirm, where more ease is waiting.

> **You have to love your reasons enough to have your own back during the squirm.**

If you find yourself in people-pleasing mode, just get lovingly curious. Perhaps it's a safe place to practice. I know when I am getting lots of opportunities to practice, it's time for me to review what my business boundaries are.

I remember it was Small Business Saturday in 2023. I don't work Saturdays, but my brain was feeding me some scarcity thoughts about how a business coach should show up on this national day for small businesses. So, against my own time-off boundaries, I showed up on social media and started to sell. For the first time ever, I had four instant inquiries about coaching. Wow! Good thing I showed up and worked, right? Not so much. But my business wanted me to practice.

Oh, what a safe place to come back into alignment. They all had interesting similarities (dressed in different outfits, of course). They all asked me questions that would have triggered my old people pleaser.

"Can I pay half now and half in the new year?" (I have a pay-in-full policy.)

"Do you have a discount?" (Not unless you are a client and get special pricing.)

"I want a conversation with you soon." (I did not have any consult appointments open.)

"My biz partner and I want to hire you as our coach." (I typically coach individually.)

I was squirming. My old people pleaser wanted to convince me to bend on every boundary I had because I must capitalize on the interest. I heard the voice of sales gurus wanting me to convert clients no matter what. I heard an inner critic telling me lies: *These are the last humans who will ever be interested*, and, *I am blowing it if I don't make it work*.

But I've come too far. I've healed too much.

Boundaries help us love one another better.

I knew that if I said yes to any one of these requests, I would set myself up for premeditated resentment. It's not the interested client's job to know my boundaries. They can ask for whatever they want to ask for. It's on me to uphold my own policies.

We are grown women. We are successful and competent. It is fascinating how it only takes one sentence in an email to kick up all our people-pleasing wounds.

I could cry for all the mental torment we go through just holding a boundary. If this is you, you are not alone. Our nervous system will get so activated that we are convinced we'd rather abandon our well-being than fail, screw it up, or have someone be mad at us.

> Bring your recovering people pleaser to your business, give her a new assignment, and then help her through it–loving yourself the whole way.

Oof. My love, I get it. My people pleaser was formed in response to trying to stay safe, and yours might also have been. This is deep stuff, and we can't gloss over the huge lift it is to regulate our nervous systems when we are triggered and in a trauma response. Get the professional support you need. And when you are ready, you can bring your recovering people pleaser to your business, give her a new assignment, and then help her through it—loving yourself the whole way.

I've promoted my people pleaser to being my Chief Compassion Officer. She used to fix all the problems, worry about everyone all the time, and hustle to avoid judgment. Now she gets to use those valuable skills to help me love and comfort myself. She's instructed to give to others from overflow and to be a helper from a place of grounded wholeness.

Visibility

Ever have a dream where you feel naked? Exposed? Sometimes, that can be how we feel when we put our services and products up for sale. Maybe the offer to help people isn't the issue, but asking for the exchange of money for your solution feels vulnerable.

When we are selling something for the first time or hundred-and-first time, it's an exercise in visibility. We live in times when we see successful business owners being trolled in comments, given one-star reviews if they step "out of line," and even being canceled. It's no wonder we can flinch when it's time to go be seen in the world.

Have you ever written a powerful post or shared a video message, then second-guessed it, deleted it, or edited it so it was more palatable? You are not alone. You are not wrong. You are seeking safety.

To grow our business, we get to partner with the squirm of being seen.

I find that most female business owners are hiding in one way or another. It's not because we want to hide; there are layers here. It may not be hard for you to share and help, but how does it feel to invite people to pay you for those solutions?

> Most female business owners are
> hiding in one way or another.

What do you notice when you think about putting your price up for everyone to see?

How about thinking about going live on social media?

Would you feel nervous standing up and giving your elevator pitch at a networking meeting?

How about setting up your first vendor table at a new event?

What thoughts start kicking in?

What do you feel in your body?

You're not doing it wrong. You have a normal nervous system situation going on.

My money coach, Serena Hicks, says, "We are the descendants of the most effective worriers." Our ability to scan for threats keeps us alive. Our nervous system can absolutely put sales into that category. And selling is being visible.

As a baseline, our normal biological imperative is to keep us alive. Keep us safe. So, each time we step out of a normal routine and do something new, we are going to have to regulate that vagus nerve of ours.

We also have years of cultural conditioning happening. If anyone you grew up learning from also commented about people being sleazy if they sell something, you have conditioning to contend with. Just like our money stories, I bet you can find a few sentences from your past that might have left unhelpful residue. Now it may be preventing you from shining as brightly as you can.

If someone has ever said some version of, "I wouldn't pay for that," on a post of yours or in person, I'm sorry. Sometimes it's family and friends. That hurts, and you're not alone. Here's what I want to invite you to do right now if a past comment has stung you.

Ask yourself these questions:

Is this truly someone who is my ideal client? (Spoiler alert: the answer is no. Your ideal clients value what you do and love to pay you.)

Is this someone living the kind of life I want to live?

Does this person share my values?

Does this person pay my bills?

Is this person also in the arena of visibility?

Is this a belief I want to carry around?

None of these immediately erase the sting of a comment, but it puts things in perspective. When we keep our eyes and hearts on the ball of who we're truly here to help, and not just try to satisfy people who will never pay us, it adds to our courage bank.

Visibility is an act of courage.

> **Our wounds may go back to a time when we heard others being judged.**

Our wounds may go back to a time when we heard others being judged. I repeatedly heard from multiple grown-ups in my young life saying, "Who does she think she is?" and "She's getting too big for her britches," when women showed up and were visible.

Visibility

Just think of how many people lose their minds when the NFL game cameras cut away to Taylor Swift in the stands.

So.

Many.

People.

None of whom are likely your customers, but I am positive millions of women subconsciously tone it down the more we see powerful humans getting ripped on for just being visible. Maybe you had a reaction too. I get it.

We can internalize this societal norm of judging those who are out there being visible and find ourselves judging other female business owners. Have you ever noticed yourself having a visceral reaction to a woman out there killin' it? I have. For sure. When we feel wobbly in some aspect of ourselves, that's likely going to be the hook that has us judging them.

> **What triggers us is always an invitation to bring something that hurts to the light so it can be loved on.**

I remember thinking and even joking that the women who seemed to have it all (the body, the money, the face, the house) must have some sort of downfall—like bad breath. I feel some guilt wash over me still, even nearly a decade later, but that's just not helpful. I can now have compassion for myself. What triggers us is always an invitation to bring something that hurts to the light so it can be loved on.

I was insecure about not being "the whole package" (mostly my body), so it came out as judgment. The antidote was that as I started to judge myself less, I started to judge other women less. The book *The Four Agreements* by Don Miguel Ruiz gave me new awareness and a new, simple code to live by.[11] I started to take nothing personally, assume the best, do my best, and be impeccable with my word. The next step was to actually get to know some of these goddesses who I would have judged. They were beautiful humans inside and out who did not deserve my judgment.

When we know better, we can do better.

This helped me heal insecurities. As it turns out, when we know better, we can do better. (Thank you, Maya Angelou.) I remember feeling so much better the next time I came across a photo of a gorgeous woman being visible, and I could truly feel happy for her.

What is your visibility judgment hook? Is it seeing someone celebrate a big money milestone? Seeing photos of a beachside retreat you would love to hold someday?

Is it seeing someone get to market first with something that feels really similar to your offer? Do you worry you'll look like you're copying someone who's in your same space? Do you feel as if people are copying you?

Let's pause and send love to the parts of us that feel wobbly and hooked. You're not doing it wrong. It's a chance to partner with your business to heal something.

Comparison rides shotgun with our visibility wound. In one of my coaching groups, I saw someone coin the word *comparanoia*, and it is a remarkable way to describe what our nervous system does as it scans for safety in a world of visibility fear. Unless we love on the parts that think we're not enough, it will burn up so much life force.

Our business is going to keep us hiding in comparanoia or judgment until we shift out of fear and into celebration, love, or understanding. If you're not ready for the "namaste" (the light in me honors the light in you sentiment), perhaps something more tactical can help.

The author of *Secrets of the Millionaire Mind*, T. Harv Eker, teaches his students to say "good for you" every time you see someone else with something you want (like a car).[12] I remember this worked well for my husband, who really wanted this specific truck. Instead of the "must be nice" reflex, he started saying, "Good for you," when he'd see this kind of truck on the highway. He didn't feel it yet but was willing to say it. Later that year, our company was able to buy that truck he wanted. He shifted from lack to abundance. It worked.

I'll never forget the day the CEO of my company sent me an email and said, "You did it!" She was referring to crossing the seven-figure mark in one year. It was the one goal I had yet to achieve. I felt the nervous system activation for sure. I also felt pride. The sad thing was, I didn't feel like I had anyone to really celebrate it with. Money was a touchy subject for my husband and me at the time, and my friends were not reaching for that kind of money goal, so it just kind of felt hollow.

In my mind, because it was such a milestone, it felt important to be visible with it. Not in a showoff way, but in an honoring way. At the time (it's a smaller percentage now), the statistic was that only 4 percent of female entrepreneurs reach that seven-figure year. I was in the business of building other business owners up, so it felt important to celebrate it. Also, I believe what we appreciate, appreciates. I wanted to give my business an attagirl.

I chose LinkedIn to mark the occasion. I found the stat about the 4 percent and crafted a nice short post about how grateful I was to have reached this milestone and thanked all of the clients and team members who made it possible.

I was being visible.

My hands shook as I posted it. But it felt like it was what I needed to do to normalize what I wanted to see more of in the world. I didn't want to shrink. I didn't want to silently go about my day as if it was just a normal Thursday or whatever it was.

So, I hit post.

And crickets.

More crickets.

My brain started to brain. Inner critic kicked in, feeding me all kinds of possibilities about being judged. Telling me it was braggy (oof, there's a visibility wound), and people would think I was rich now (we were and we weren't, if you know what I mean).

I wanted to delete it. But my growth edge was clear. Own it. For myself. Not for anyone else. It still stings a bit to think about how flat that post was.

The wisdom in me understands that I nailed the assignment, though. I showed up shaking. Owned my truth. Did what I'd encourage a client to do (celebrate), and I got the memo. The million-dollar year was for me. To prove to myself that it could be done. My capacity to be visible even when no one else was cheering expanded. That was healing. I don't need anyone to clap. I keep showing up for myself. If it helps someone else, great. If I get a lesson wrapped in crickets, so be it.

I did make a decision that day, though. I would make sure to clap hard when I saw someone brave enough to celebrate milestones. They publish a book? I celebrate. They hit a new revenue amount? I cheer. They take a vacay? I'm saying, "Yes, queen!"

> **Each time we can find a way to celebrate another business owner who is out there crushing it, we expand our capacity to win too.**

Each time we can find a way to celebrate another business owner who is out there crushing it, we expand our capacity to win too. In many coaching circles, I've heard, "If it's possible for one of us, it's possible for all of us." That's a great mantra on our road to expanding our capacity to show up and shine.

Limiting Beliefs

Did you notice how, from the moment you shared that you wanted to start a business, every human had opinions about it? The projections begin immediately. Your grandpappy's beliefs, your mama's money fears, your friend's insecurities—here they come.

Everything you've ever heard about money, success, and dreaming big will be like a suggested playlist on YouTube. Some input will be helpful and enjoyable; some will be better skipped. But depending on our wounding, we'll often take those beliefs and adopt them. Maybe internalize them or rebel against them, but we'll have a reaction. And that's just other people's opinions.

You have your own onboard playlist of limiting beliefs programmed in. You've been practicing them for decades by now. And yet, when you flip your "Open for Business" sign on, you are supposed to magically overcome all those unhelpful beliefs and be a raging success.

Many books have been written about this, so I don't have to reinvent the wheel here. Just be aware that the limiting beliefs we have internalized and adopted as our own are going to stick around and be sand in the gears of living the life you want and having the business you want until you bring them up to the light.

> **Limiting beliefs are the phrases formed indirectly from the wounds of our friends and family or some other influential person in our lives.**

Limiting beliefs are the phrases formed indirectly from the wounds of our friends and family or some other influential person in our lives.

Have you ever heard or repeated one of these?

"You gotta work hard to be successful."

"Most businesses don't survive five years."

"If you want something done right, do it yourself."

I'm sure I did. I know I heard it over and over again from my dad. Some become so common, like "Money doesn't grow on trees," that you will have an entire culture swearing by it. Not one of these uplifts us.

It is absolutely FREE to believe in your dreams.

It is absolutely EXPENSIVE to believe in the limits of other people's thoughts.

Limiting beliefs are not facts. So, we get to take them to court. Shine a light and see if there is any real evidence there.

Think about a limiting belief you may have riding around in the back of your brain. I've heard everything from "I'm terrible at this," "I can't delegate this yet" to "I'm not good at finishing things" to "I'm not a legitimate business owner." They are infinite. Go gently, as these may be tied to old trauma.

What is a repeated thought that shows up in your brain? (If you are stuck finding it, just think back to the last time you were frustrated or wanted to finish something but didn't; there is probably a limiting belief in there.)

Ask yourself these questions:

Is this even true?

What is actually true instead?

Is this what I believe?

Is this what I want to continue to believe?

Would I have someone paint this on my conference room wall?

Would I get this tattooed for inspiration?

Is this even mine? If not, whose voice do I hear when I think this thought?

After you find that person, ask yourself, would you want them to be CEO of your company?

Would you want them to give the annual motivational speech to your team?

Limiting Beliefs

It's not even about them, but the answer is usually no. When we uncover our limiting beliefs, we can actually do something about them. Get coached on it; give yourself ample, written evidence of what is true. Yes, write that evidence down! Finish a marketing post? Write it down as win. Send the invoice and receive the payment? Write it down. Say no to a "should"? Boom. Write it down. Celebrate every single successful move in the direction of your dreams.

> Congratulate yourself for being willing to evolve.

And congratulate yourself for being willing to evolve. Your life does get a lot juicier on the other side of squirming through forming new beliefs.

Unlike our friends and family who don't own a business, we are willing to look. Nothing gets you willing to figure out what's throttling your success like needing to make a business succeed. We are willing to learn about mindset, get therapy, get coaching, get a room of peers to share with, and even get physically healthier so our businesses work better.

Notice where you're telling yourself a story. Take it to court. Track the evidence of what is true. Celebrate, celebrate, celebrate. Dissolve one limiting belief at a time and replace it with more helpful truth about who you really are. This is how it's done.

> **If you haven't lately–or ever–give yourself a freakin' pat on the back for signing up for this brave thing we call business growth!**

If you haven't lately—or ever—give yourself a freakin' pat on the back for signing up for this brave thing we call business growth!

Workaholism

Just as with limiting beliefs, we can bring old ways of working to our business. When you're busy grinding, you can go years on pure adrenaline and dreams. Many will applaud you if you are the hardest worker in a traditional workplace. You might even get employee of the month recognition. Then, you try to translate that to business, and eventually, you look around and wonder where it went wrong.

It's socially acceptable to be a hustler or an achiever in entrepreneurship too. You're probably making money, winning awards, and getting gold stars from people who are used to patriarchy-approved pushing.

Then, somewhere along the ride of high achieving, you start to notice the wins don't feel as awesome as you thought they would. Maybe you hit milestones and don't get a rush or feel like celebrating them anymore. You might reach new heights of revenue or build a big team and wonder why none of it feels satisfying. Maybe you look around, and there's no one to really celebrate with because you've been so independent and isolated.

As you grow your business, nothing is as easy as burning that candle at both ends until you're burned all the way out. Ask me how I know. Being the achiever serves us well—until it doesn't. It might have made you the golden child in your career or in your family growing up, but it can get out of hand as a business owner.

Why?

Because the opportunities to grind, build, and create are 24/7. Endless chances to blow past our own needs. You don't ever have to turn it off. And if you end up treating yourself to some time away, how many of us take email (and all the stress) on vacation? Yikes.

At some point, there are diminishing returns on your hustle, and your workaholism becomes a liability, not an asset. Maybe it's your spouse or your kid who feels as though the business is more important than they are. Maybe it's a two-by-four from the universe, and your body is screaming for a break. Maybe a bestie taps you on the shoulder and says, "Are you sure this is worth it?"

Whomever the messenger is, thank them. They might have just saved your business.

For me, it took hallucinating in my kitchen before I was ready to reform my workaholic ways. I was standing at my glass-top stove, working after my babies were asleep, trying to meet the print deadline for our magazine. I looked down at the rubber mat I was standing on, and it looked as if I were suspended in space instead of standing on my kitchen floor. I was dizzy and disoriented. I thought, *Am I going crazy?*

Turns out, I was burned out. Fried.

I invested in a life coach who introduced me to the concepts that would help me find more balance.

Looking back, I am smirking because I know I wasn't hiring her for my body's well-being. I was hiring her to make sure I could still run my business. Oh, priorities. Thank you, business. It unlocked a realization that my personal well-being is the well-being of my business, not the other way around.

I can say with confidence I have healed my workaholism wound. I now work two days a week, and I take the summer off, aside from a handful of hours spent coaching my Should Free Six Figures group.

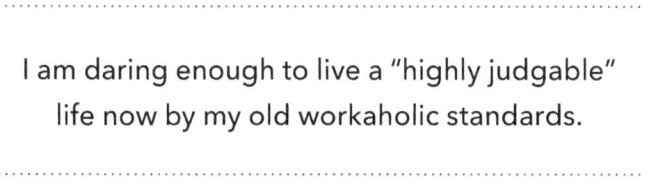

I am daring enough to live a "highly judgable" life now by my old workaholic standards.

I am daring enough to live a "highly judgable" life now by my old workaholic standards. Ten-years-ago me would have looked at me today and wondered, *Who the heck is this lady?* She has no tolerance for hustle, she's taking long naps, and is lounging on her dock at the lake home she only dreamed about having at retirement. My business helped me heal.

How can you shift out of something like workaholism? (Without needing a two-by-four?) You have to find a reward that's bigger. Bigger than the payoff you get by staying in task mode.

For me, that was dangling the carrot of little joys.

I wrote this note to my email community a couple of years back, when I was still just taking July off, not the bulk of the summer, yet. It sums it up nicely:

> I learned how to say no so I could say yes.
>
> I got to do my favorite job this week.
>
> Boat captain.
>
> There is no greater summer fun for me than to see my daughter and one of her friends with smiles that make their cheeks hurt, bouncing across the wake and waves on a tube.
>
> It's hard to beat.
>
> I laugh.
>
> They squeal.
>
> The boat engine roars.
>
> It's been my favorite yes this week.
>
> But I had to figure out how to say a lot of no's to get to a place where I can say yes to a sleepover for my ten-year-old on a Wednesday.
>
> I have been working on it for years.
>
> It led to a pinnacle.
>
> I discovered from my friend Allison that you can take an entire month off if you want.
>
> Be still, my recovering workaholic heart.
>
> Say WHAAAT?
>
> It was a goal of mine four years ago.

This is the third July I've said no to working and yes to summer fun.

I know we're only a couple of days in.

Yes, I do keep communication efforts going for The Juicy Good Life, and I keep in touch with my Should Free Six Figures program members, but the in-person meetings and Zoom calls, etc. stop until the second week of August.

What I notice is that I'm more "Sarah" than I am "business coach" when I give myself extended periods of time off. It keeps me in the yes mode my kids dream of . . . the adventurous mom who goes swimming all the time and does cannonball contests.

I love it.

To get here, I had to say no to guilt, obligation, procrastination, hiding, playing small, avoiding, and fearing the judgment of others.

The part of my brain that said it's all going to fall apart if I take a month off? It just needed a plan.

And that plan needed follow-through.

Before I did this for the first time in 2021, I got coached up big-time.

It meant I needed to be on the ball with my schedule, revenue, and systems leading up to my month off. At that time, I had a marketing agency with a lot of moving parts, as well as my business coaching practice.

I'm so glad I took the leap.

I'm so glad I got coaching for my worries.

I'm so glad I showed up as the woman who can be the kick-butt business owner and the summer-adventure mom.

You get to have whatever is on your heart.

You just need to learn what you're saying no to . . .

So you can say that HELL YES to your dream.

What is it for you that has you putting off your dream life?

In these past ten years, I've squirmed a lot as I've deleted nearly all the "shoulds," reformed my limiting beliefs, and leaned into believing every dream I have is possible. It's possible not through overworking, but through the positive impact I create for my clients.

Instead of limiting beliefs and long hours, I've implemented my Peaceful Planner process, power thoughts (thoughts that help us create the results we want), and being true to myself. I now follow inspiration instead of to-do lists. I can live this way because of all the healing my business has inspired in me and a whole lotta designing a life I can call juicy good.

> **Everything you want is on the other side of some squirm.**

Everything you want is on the other side of some squirm. Every year, I help clients set up their lives so it actually works. No, you don't have to sacrifice revenue. I consistently celebrate with clients who have record revenue as they work fewer and fewer hours.

What kind of freedom would be worth the squirm of rearranging how and when you work?

What fun do you always put off because of work?

Where are you seeing diminishing returns in your business because you're tired?

What could be possible in your business if you recharged more?

How would your life improve if you believed anything was possible for your schedule?

I designed the Peaceful Planner process, which is the container for the life you want. I typically reserve it for clients of mine or members of Should Free Six Figures, but check my website when you find this book to see if there are options available for you to experience the Peaceful Planner process. **www.thejuicygoodlife.com**

Money

Every wound we've explored so far could be at play when it comes to how we manage money in our business.

Money and people-pleasing? You betcha.

Generational trauma? Riding shotgun.

Limiting beliefs and painful patterns? A daily thing.

Healing our money wounds goes hand in hand with building a satisfying, sustainable business. The bigger you want your bottom line to get, the more important it is to heal your "stuff" around money. You won't have to look far; I'm sure something has come up today that wants to be healed. Maybe it was the story you told yourself when you opened your bank app or the reason you gave yourself to not show up and sell something.

We all have money wounds that could suck the joy out of our days. Maybe this is the thing you feel most insecure about or that causes fights. Maybe you have trouble receiving it at all.

Ask yourself the important questions you're practicing with me already.

What story is my brain telling me about money?

What am I making my current money circumstance mean about me?

What part of me needs to be loved?

What kind of relationship do I want to have with money?

Do I believe it's possible?

What would have to happen to have this kind of relationship with money?

What hurts from the past are ready for healing?

I feel deep gratitude that I can reflect in this way with you. It shows how far we can come in our healing process. Healing our money story is powerful and potent. After my parents' divorce, my mom went back to school, and we were scraping by. I will never forget counting food stamps (they used to come in printed coupon books, back in the day) to get organized for a late-night grocery run—so no one would see us using food stamps.

It's amazing, but we always had enough. I never went hungry. I learned to figure it out by watching my mom figure it out. Both parents were always willing to do what it takes, and that stuck with me. I worked several jobs in high school so I could buy the clothes that would conceal the fact that I was the free lunch kid. Twenty years later, that free lunch kid would create a million-dollar-plus year in business—something only 1.9 percent of female business owners accomplish, according to a 2024 article in Forbes.[13]

My belief that it could be achieved had to be bigger than my wound. I am grateful that I've had no money. I'm grateful that I had to hustle in our first business to even sell fifty-dollar ads. I'm grateful that I got to see with my own eyes that a million-dollar year doesn't make your money problems disappear.

Your relationship with that money is what matters, not the amount.

Your relationship with that money is what matters, not the amount. But I had to get there to see it myself. My seven-figure clients say that too. We're all proud of the accomplishment and grateful to do it, but unless we have healed our money stuff, that number is just another number to kick up more worry.

I've invested well over what I paid for my private college degree to learn how to grow my business and be a better money magnet. I have made money, spent money, and rented money—to the tune of millions generated and millions out the door in expenses and overhead. I have been both debt-free and up to my eyeballs in it several times now.

I was no more relaxed when I had all my debt paid off because I was always hyper-focused on staying out of debt. I didn't even enjoy those debt-free times. I gave money so much power over my first ten years of business that this year (2025), I finally said to my coach, "I'm done making debt repayment my personality."

Because my business is ready for me to heal the wound that says I have to "get it right." Getting money "right" is riddled with patriarchal and cultural conditioning that I just have no time for anymore. I am done giving over my power to money. I am choosing to be in a new relationship with it. I make lovely amounts of money that takes care of my family. My soul does not care if I have debt; old conditioning and wounding does.

> **I am done giving over my power to money. I am choosing to be in a new relationship with it.**

This is my new level. My new layer of healing my money wound. The truth is, we're always evolving in our relationship with money when we're healing. There are new layers and new seasons that call for new ways of partnering with money.

You might be in a season of seeing how much you can **create**.

You might be in a season of seeing how much you can **leverage**.

You might be in a season of seeing how much you can **save**.

What season are you in right now?

Despite our programming, there's no one right way to do money.

The aligned way is where you can be yourself, with a mostly regulated nervous system, and use it as a resource to live the way you want to live.

In a voice memo just this week, one of my clients who is healing her money stuff cried gratitude tears that she now sees she's always had more than enough. That her decisions to invest in herself didn't ruin anything as fear implied it would. She has grown her business by 35 percent, hitting record revenue each year, and continues to see that money is a tool, not a weapon. She is no longer looking for evidence to prove her core wound right. She sees money as a partner now.

It's pretty amazing to watch women's money wounds heal in real time. We always have decision-making power. We can keep it simple and remember our thoughts about money can shut us down or help us shine.

Instagram shows us the women out there in the spotlight, with money to burn on whatever they are doing. They unapologetically sell, shop, educate, dance, travel, pitch, solve, and entertain. Our brains tell us they have a money formula figured out that we don't yet.

What have they figured out? A decision.

They've decided to shine.

I bet they have vastly different amounts of money.

But they shine anyway.

We spend most of our time telling our money it is not enough.

Not growing enough.

Not coming in fast enough.
Not keeping enough of it.
Not giving us enough relief.

My money coach helped me create a new way to relate to money. By using sweet examples like little kids and puppies, she helped the concept truly land. Serena Hicks would remind us that we would never talk to a little child or a puppy the way we talk to our money.

Think about it. Would you ever look at a little child or a puppy and tell them how they aren't enough? That you hate managing them? That you wish you didn't even have to deal with them? That they aren't moving fast enough? That they are so frustrating. That you are terrible with them? Or, flat out avoid and neglect them.

Makes ya kinda sad, right?

> Money is an energy. It wants to partner with you.

Yet we do this with money all the time. And expect more to come to us. To somehow just trust us. Money is an energy. It wants to partner with you. It wants to help you. To make you proud. Just like a little kid or a puppy, it wants to feel good and safe with you too.

How often are we really hard on our money (and let's go ahead and say hard on ourselves here too)? The answer is: we can be pretty damn harsh.

You're not a puppy-shaming Cruella. You are an incredible human with a heart of gold. Your business is here to be your best friend. Your money wants to be in partnership with you too. It just needs to be noticed for all the ways it IS there for you.

> **Your business is here to be your best friend. Your money wants to be in partnership with you too.**

Do you get to pick up your kids and design your day the way you want?

Do you get to feed your fur baby without thinking twice?

Do you get to have lunch with friends on a whim?

Do you have more than enough for today?

Do you have more than enough to pay for this book?

Yes.

Yet when was the last time you intentionally thanked your money?

What I have noticed is that when we celebrate every single ounce of freedom, joy, and opportunity it creates, our money meets us with more. More winning. More "Yay" moments.

Pretty soon, your brain understands the assignment. You form new neuropathways that are wired not to just watch for threats but to watch for wins.

You start to show up more energized. More energy creates more magnetism for what you want. And the best cycle begins. The one where you are more aligned with your money.

To start being in a more harmonious relationship with your money, let's get lovingly curious:

Where are you being hard on your money?

Where are you ignoring it?

What wound is trying to be healed when you're mean to money?

What does that hurt need from you now?

What would your ideal relationship with money look like?

How would you know you're in that kind of relationship with money? What would be happening in your daily life?

What would your top three values help you decide about money?

When you set money goals, what story will you tell yourself, or what will your brain say to you if you don't reach them?

What would you like to pay yourself this year?

What would you like to save this year?

Money

What would you like to invest in this year?

Where does your money show up in the best ways for you?

Where do you feel in alignment with money?

What do you want to remember (with love) the next time you are faced with your money wound?

Purchases

The "shoulds" we buy can drive us right into the red on our bank balance. They can also finally lead us to freedom if we let them. You see, for years, and sometimes still to this day, I will be tempted to buy the sexy business solutions.

They used to come from older dudes who are excellent at marketing simplistic strategies. Because they do have it figured out. For them. And they package it nicely and neatly. Just like our brains like it. Just do X, and you'll get Y.

....

> The "shoulds" we buy can drive us right into the red on our bank balance.

....

But those are hamster wheels that end up being engines of frustration. And I have spent tens of thousands of dollars chasing those hacks. Some worked. I love a good system. I've learned from it all. But until we start to filter out what is a true *desire* and what is a *should*, we slow our growth.

Don't worry, you haven't done it wrong. Everything is a lesson. Even the stuff that we want to feel bad about buying. This is a new invitation to look at our purchases from a place of empowerment instead of not-enough-ness.

> **Until we start to filter out what is a *desire* and what is a *should*, we slow our growth.**

Paying for support because you truly want that support? Game-changer.

Buying a book that gets you one step closer to understanding your life better? Yummy.

Throwing money at a well-marketed, sexy solution you never use? Energy drain.

Reflexively hitting the buy button because cheap dopamine feels so good for a moment? Understandable.

We've all done it. Heck, as I admitted before, I still sometimes do it. And you know what? There are programs I bought years ago that are finally ready for me to enjoy them. They are outliers. That's okay. The trick is to not use it as a weapon. To not make yourself wrong for it. But we do want to be awake to it so we can make room for more of what we want in our lives.

To help make some room for more joy, let's release guilt over purchases and programs that may live rent-free in your

Purchases

head. You know, the ones you use as a weapon? I have a few biggies that haunt me.

The temptation often centers around my old pattern of guilt trips and what I "should" do to be a "good business owner" who's "good with money." I used to force myself to do that program just because I bought it. It wouldn't care if it was outdated. I only wanted to avoid feeling the squirm of "wasting" that money. Not anymore. I have the best news. Even your "wasted" money can be a catalyst for healing.

That $6,000 leadership training I bought for my CEO and me? We didn't do it.

Why? Because the healing truly came from letting go of something I was trying to force.

"This will fix it," is a red flag thought for me now. I didn't know it then. I thought I was being a supportive employer who values growth. (I was, and I do.)

> **It's never about the action. It's always about the motive or intention that drives it.**

But it's never about the action. It's always about the motive or intention that drives it. I was in reflexive, fix-it mode at the time. It was a total gift that my team member never opened the heavy, gold-and-black book that came with that course. It lived on her bookshelf until her last day, when I got it back. Then, it lived on my bookshelf as I continued to be in fix-it mode with my marketing agency. It was a tangible representation of what wasn't working. We didn't need more tactics. The writing was on the wall.

So that $6,000 course that could be a shame bomb? It was a gift. It was part of a mountain of evidence piling up that showed me that I was out of alignment. I was trying to take my business to the emergency room when it was ready for the funeral home.

Pretty deep for a course purchase, right?

I love to be dramatic for effect.

In reality, when you buy things out of "should" energy, it will quickly feel off. Let your business help you heal this old pattern. Let your business show you what it wants for you.

> **Let your business show you what it wants for you.**

But we have to open our eyes. What red flags can you watch for when you're buying to get a fix (solutions or dopamine)? As you look at your purchases (gentle reminder that this is a tool, not a weapon or shame-and-blame material), what purchases moved you closer to the life you want?

Let's celebrate them here:

Great job.

Now, let's look at what it was about that purchase that helped the most. List that to the right of your items on the previous page. Did it get you unstuck? Did it help you think of a new idea? Did it remind you that you tend to buy things when you are in PMS? (Oops, ha ha, maybe that's just me.)

I invite you to go deeper and riff on the questions below so your wisdom can integrate.

How were you divinely guided when saying yes to those purchases?

How could that same wisdom serve you as you move forward?

What wise questions can you ask yourself next time you're invited or intrigued to buy support? (Example: Does this get me closer to or further away from my goals?)

Receiving

"You have to become a bigger vessel, Sarah." Those words from my first spiritual mentor, Aveen, triggered me at the time. She was in my life to help me grow, and she had a way of knowing exactly what was up for me to heal. She was helping me through my money wounds at the time. Being the wise soul that she is, she knew I was missing a big piece around money.

I was the go-getter, make-it-happen lady. I was really good at creating and selling, but she saw through my surface struggles. I wanted to make more money. I'd paid off more than six figures of debt in six months, but I wanted to feel better. Turns out, being debt-free was not as delicious as I'd dreamed it to be, and my brain wanted to hit the next level of achievement. At the time, I hadn't crested a million-dollar year but had gotten so close for so many years. I wanted more money, and I wanted it yesterday.

However, instead of talking about what makes more cash, she talked about my capacity to receive. I didn't love it. We don't usually love what's ready to be healed. I was squirming, and it was simmering in my brain, leaving me annoyed.

She tried to help me see the yin and yang of masculine and feminine energy, that to be in harmony with what I wanted to create next, I needed to see that important flow between giving and receiving. Receiving didn't compute as important yet.

My achievements had me tied up in my ego. "I was a big enough vessel," my brain snorted back silently. I did nothing with her advice at first, but her words, "become a bigger vessel," were like an alarm—coming in loud every so often—but I just kept hitting snooze.

Giving is way safer than receiving.

Maybe you're like me. Giving is way safer than receiving. We get to feel good about ourselves, we get the dopamine hit of doing nice things for others, and we don't have to feel beholden to anyone. Winning, right?

Sigh.

You know those wise mentors of ours? They usually know where to aim the flashlight, illuminating what we'd rather keep in the dark. She saw through my rugged independence and knew what was holding me back from feeling like I could welcome in more abundance. Until I learned how to be in a reciprocal relationship with giving and receiving, I would stay stagnant.

I found a receiving wound. I am still working through it, but I am a bigger vessel now after years of practicing in safe ways with safe people. You see, it was baked into my being from youth that receiving wasn't safe. It wasn't love; it was leverage. It wasn't just strings attached; it was barbed wire. To receive meant to brace for the day the "gift" or act of service was thrown back in your face to guilt you with it.

I saw it span generations. My grandfather kept a list of "gifts" right down to firewood for my parents and laundry detergent he gave my cousin. If anyone got out of line, he'd say a mean thing about all he had done for them to shame them into submission.

So, I became the lady who only gave—and didn't receive unless absolutely forced. Much safer, right? To our wounded self, yes. But to your *soul* that wants you to heal, it's a barrier between you and the people who want to do nice things for you.

> To your *soul* that wants you to heal, it's a barrier between you and the people who want to do nice things for you.

I'll never forget my forty-fifth birthday week. My besties were divinely sent to help me heal. I bet yours are too. They know me well.

They understand it practically takes an arm-wrestling match with me over the tab for lunch. They know I squirm when I receive. But this particular birthday week cracked me open in the best way.

My bestie, Rachelle, took me camping, floating, and waterfall chasing—on top of gifting me pedis and lunches. That would have been enough, but nope, she and I joined my "treat-yourself Jedi" friend Jodi. She took me on a choose-your-adventure day, with all the things our grownup selves don't usually indulge in, like cake shopping and adventure scavenger hunt complete with permanent friendship bracelets. I felt my body and brain get triggered about two hours into this Sunday fun day, and yet the spoiling continued. I had reached my "upper limit," as Gay Hendricks writes about in *The Big Leap*.[14]

We need to remember with compassion where the wound formed.

I was fully squirming with each new treat on this day of receiving. My wound didn't know the difference between old pain and new safety. It's embarrassing to say I squirmed the whole day because how silly it is that getting gifts would be so triggering. But we need to remember with compassion where the wound formed. That was a tender and scared young me who saw what she needed to do to be safe in her family.

I know it's safe with my besties and that when I can receive from safe people, it rewires that old fear in my brain. My wound heals. I become a bigger vessel. I create more capacity to experience more abundance in other ways, especially in my business.

Do you feel challenged receiving?

When was the last time you received something without feeling as if you needed to reciprocate?

Who are the safe people in your life you'd like to practice receiving from?

What could it mean for your life and business if you expanded your capacity to receive?

What does becoming a bigger vessel look like for you?

What abundance would you experience?

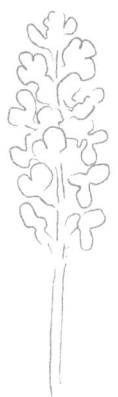

Right on Time

No matter what wounds our business kicks up to help us heal, each frustration and each challenge are sacred messengers. They are here to help us see something. Something that wants to be loved on so you can keep peeling away the armor that weighs you down.

There is a phrase that helps my clients take their power back. It's only three words long, but it keeps them more grounded than anything else. Those words?

Right.

On.

Time.

What typically happens is a business owner will make an empowered decision in her business. Let's just say that it's choosing to raise her prices. She feels good about it and changes those prices on her website. That will be the moment she comes across a comment on a social media thread about so-and-so raising prices, and who does she think she is charging that . . . yadda, yadda.

Right on time.

> **Each frustration and each challenge are sacred messengers.**

Maybe a client decides to sell her company, and she's done her work on what she would like to sell it for. That's when she'll meet someone whose sister just had to close because she couldn't sell it, and they'll tell her how bad the market is and how no one has money right now. They'll wish her the best but tell her to not hold her breath.

Right on time.

I know a client is making huge progress when she calls it out for what it is. If she laughs when she tells me what happened "right on time," I know healing is underway.

If you find yourself here, you get to take comfort in knowing nothing has gone wrong. It's those old familiar wounds just looking to get reassurance from your newfound confidence.

Why? Brains be brainin'. Your brain prefers the familiar old fear over new scary growth, even if it hurts.

Once you realize what's happening, you don't have to unconsciously hand over your power to the fear. You get to look this opportunity to practice square in the face and not be as wobbly. It's right on time. You get to practice being the person who trusts herself. This is the best result I see my clients get from doing this healing work. They learn to really trust themselves. They lead themselves first.

> **Your brain prefers the familiar old fear over new scary growth, even if it hurts.**

We are never done healing. We are always in new seasons of life with new opportunities to practice being who we want to be. Running a business from this more healed version of ourselves is never done. Instead of that process feeling daunting, you can look forward to meeting the next version of you. She's amazing. You'll love her.

We're Never Done

There's a potentially frustrating realization that happens along the healing path. It's that there is no finish line. There's no magical day when there will be nothing left to work on.

Just a new layer to love on. A new wounded part you'll meet that needs connection. A new numbing mechanism.

> There's no magical day when there
> will be nothing left to work on.

A new level of money to learn how to partner with. A new spot where you feel unprepared. A new expansion to squirm through. I'm sorry to break it to you. We just keep evolving, apparently. (Weak chuckles and cringe face.)

I was annoyed by this for approximately 7.4 of my 11 years in business. I was fully convinced there would be magic, and I'd never think about money again when I hit a $1 million year. I believed if I could just get one more leadership training, I'd finally get it "right."

I was sure that if our team could just care as much as I did about finishing that sales funnel, we could actually relax. I was in what I call the when/then life.

When I reach this (fill-in-the-blank metaphorical destination or task achieved in the future), *then* I'll feel (fill-the-blank sense of relief, happiness, accomplishment).

> **The when/then life keeps us hopping, but it does not bring us healing.**

The when/then life keeps us hopping, but it does not bring us healing. When we think there's a finish line, we'll just keep pushing and running for it, looking for the black-and-white checkered flag that will finally give us a break. So, how do we know when we're out of when/then and instead we're healing?

It's when we spend days, not weeks, replaying that thing we did that made us cringe. When we open that bank app and don't make the number mean anything about our worthiness as a human. When we hear a potential customer say, "No thanks," and we agree that they may be better served elsewhere.

It's when we show up shaking at a new event, and we aren't mean to ourselves for bumbling over our pitch. When we wake up and do a little happy dance as we're brushing our teeth because today, we're going to live another day of our dream, however imperfectly.

It's when we can look back on something that felt impossible years ago and see that we're actually doing it now. It's when we can be present to the goodness of now.

Befriending the Squirm

Becoming Ourselves

Why am I already getting weepy? Because I've spent hours upon hours writing about wounds and the hardest stuff we'll go through in business, but on the other side of all that squirm is—becoming more YOU.

(Fully bawling now.)

We are often so weighed down in our wounds and the daily fires of business that we don't even know who we are anymore. We take everything so seriously because it's tied to our reputation and our money. We are suffocating under the pressures of perception.

The beautiful thing is, your business will not only have you meet all your wounds so you can heal, it also wants to help you meet more joy so you can heal. Yes, joy is a healing teacher too. But only if we keep opening to it.

Joy used to feel like a far-off, maybe even nerdy concept to me. Like something reserved for the lyrics of a Christmas hymn. I was way too cool (aka "professional") sometimes to have joy.

I took myself so seriously. Even my happiness moments were rooted in success, measured by gold stars, not the glimmers of joy.

Joy was squirmy.

It turns out, the divine wisdom of my business would send me on a joy journey. It would come in the form of observing joy first. I would see it in women I got to meet and stories I got to cover for my magazine. Then, one day, it would come in the form of a primate.

> **The divine wisdom of my business would send me on a joy journey.**

Remember I owned a magazine? One month, I decided to cover my life coach's laughter yoga class as a story. (She's also my medical doctor.) Dr. Jodi Ritsch is known as The Joyful Doc, and she understood long before I did that joy is the best medicine.

I was going to be the writer and the photographer for my magazine article. I got to the laughter yoga location and had a good time watching these grown women be silly. I was on the job, trying to capture the perfect photo for the article.

Then, she asked me to participate.

Cringe.

My professional self was more than happy to smile back as these women made the "ha ha ha, ho ho ho" noises and got sillier by the second, but ME talking like an alien trying to describe a fender bender? (Yes, that was one of the prompts.) Um, no thanks.

By this time, Dr. Jodi and I had become way more than a coach and client. She was becoming a best friend. I wasn't about to say no to my friend's request. But my ego was not happy about it. I was stiff as a board as we rubbed invisible "laugh lotion" on ourselves. Playing along just enough to get by. Until the last exercise. That one changed my whole life.

Not only did my abs get a workout, but so did a part of me that had only been let out to play within my inner circle every few years. The part of me that couldn't stop laughing.

I know, I know, it's called laughter yoga. But what rose from within me was a joyful spirit. A break from holding the world's problems. A respite for a girl who shouldered way too much and a grown woman who didn't learn to be wild and uninhibited.

This business assignment led me to a place inside me that was truly free.

Free from the fear of judgment from others.

Free from being serious.

Free from having a plan.

Free from taking care of it all.

As I lay on the floor, my rigid professionalism melted into puddles of pure bliss when the breakthrough happened. The group was totally rocking the final exercise (which was to make animal noises).

> My rigid professionalism melted into puddles of pure bliss when the breakthrough happened.

I heard one of the women howl like a wolf.
I laughed.
I heard another woman make chicken noises.
I laughed harder.
Yet another decided to chime in as a rooster.
More belly laughs.
I was having such a good time. I was full on cackling.
Then I let it loose. My biggest, most ridiculous . . .
Gorilla.
Orangutang.
Chimpanzee.

I lost myself in the pure delight of it all. I laughed so hard, maybe harder than I've ever laughed in my whole life. Surrounded by a zooful of utter ridiculous noise, I found joy at full volume.

I met a part of me I didn't know yet. It unlocked a new awareness that there was more to life than having it all "under control." I am forever grateful my business helped me meet *me* that day. It took Dr. Jodi to introduce me to this new version of myself, but I never forgot that feeling of being present to joy. To the part of me capable of relaxing into it. Thank you, friend.

Now, joy is a guiding light. A nonnegotiable in my life. I didn't get here immediately. It has taken many more years of healing to let more of that version of me lead the way. To let joy be a driving force in my business and my personal life.

It unlocked a new awareness that there was more to life than having it all "under control."

I'm so much more attuned to joy that I can find it in quiet moments on my dock watching the loons dive wondering where they will pop up, adventures with my bestie on a coastal road trip, nights at the ballparks watching my kids play, and tiny don't-blink-or-you'll-miss-it miracles in nature.

I find it everywhere.

"Be joyful" is now my leading life goal.

I want joy to help us heal too.

Worth the Payoffs

When something feels hard, we have to find a payoff that's worth it. The juice has to be worth the squeeze, or we won't want to show up for the challenge. When we allow our business to help us heal, the payoffs are endless. We are going to look at all the reasons this business and personal growth is worth the squirm.

Instead of burning up precious life force resisting what it shows you, when you partner with your beautiful business, the ripple is endless. Being more *you* is the most efficient way to create a business that is sustainable.

Feeling free helps everything flow. Learning what isn't yours to hold/fix/do is wisdom that will create the energy you need. When you can consciously *choose* instead of unconsciously react, the entire game changes. When you can move through challenges with more ease, you get so much bandwidth back for what really matters to you.

> **The juice has to be worth the squeeze, or we won't want to show up for the challenge.**

When you see progress, you build confidence. Confidence creates the decisions and actions that produce the results you want. You expand your capacity for joy, love, abundance, and freedom. You honor your soul. You can make the impact you want to make.

Sound worth it?

Worth the squirm?

Yep.

How juicy are you willing to let life get?

Efficiency

Strategically speaking, the ROI (return on investment) for healing through the squirm won't be found in any business-building books (until now!) because it's always about time management.

You know what's amazing at creating time-management solutions? De-shoulding your entire operation. Turns out, what burns time is chasing what's not yours to do. You know what really helps with dropping the shoulds? Healing your wounds.

Shoulds are the things we think we have to do but aren't actually in alignment for us. So many of my clients are neurodiverse or are visionaries who grew up trying to bend to the will of a system that was full of shoulds that were not right for them.

Now we're grown—with businesses and lives and responsibilities—and those piles of shoulds are a burnout bomb waiting to go off. I bet you would be amazed if you added up all the hours you spend doing (or worrying) about crap you don't even want to do.

> **Shoulds are the things we think we have to do but aren't actually in alignment for us.**

It is a smart and strategic move to be yourself. I'm more than a decade into healing through the squirm of becoming myself, but wow, am I more efficient now than I ever was.

I built bigger and bigger business machines to handle more and more shoulds. I kicked so much butt in business, it was amazing. But I was just busy. Busy being what everyone needed me to be. I was an incredible strategist. Was a visionary who could get things done. Loved seeing all the ways I could win.

And, with the bigger machine I built to handle more shoulds, I just had to run faster to stay ahead. I was feeding the dragon. I had to hire more nannies help to cover me, more personal assistants, cleaning help, and way more salaried team members to pump out more productivity. But the more I learned about who I am becoming, the more I realized I can make the impact I want to make for the world now in a couple of days a week. I can be the mom who can go to everything. I can be the lady on her dock all summer. I can be the woman in the woods taking pictures of cool mushrooms. That is who I am now. I once was:

A successful TV anchor.

A magazine publisher.

The leader on the philanthropic boards.

A marketing agency owner.

I was good at all of them. I'm good at a lot of things I don't do anymore. I've healed into a truer, more peaceful version of me. The alignment of being true to ourselves is the highest form of ROI. My profit margins are so much better too. Shoulds are expensive!

> **The alignment of being true to ourselves is the highest form of ROI.**

When you allow your business to be your healing and de-shoulding partner, there is massive freedom to be had. When you de-should, time freedom is just one payoff.

My clients resonate deeply with the mantra we have in Should Free Six Figures: **No cages**. If you didn't want to get in the box of how it "should" be done, you were probably hard-pressed to find a place that honored your rhythms throughout your life. I'm sorry for that. I dedicate my days to helping women just like you heal from all the ways "shoulds" have stolen years of our lives. But we don't focus on the past; we tune in to the future your soul wants.

When you heal through the squirm of releasing how it "should be done," you will find so much delight in the freedom to be you.

Your business can make your big dreams real.

Your business can match your changing energy.

Your business gets to evolve with your seasons of life.
Your business can be a container for joy instead of a cage.

....

> **Your business can be a container
> for joy instead of a cage.**

....

Your business can make you money even when you abandon all the old rules.

The only thing between you and that freedom is the squirm.

Getting Paid and Loving It

Have you ever had a moment where you realized you get paid to do what you love? If you haven't slowed down enough to experience it yet, or it hasn't happened yet, the next time someone pays your invoice or hits purchase, take a moment and thank yourself.

It takes a lot of guts to start a business.

When was the last time you sat with that? Have you ever given yourself a pat on the back? Now might be a great time to write a love letter to *yourself*. We send congratulations notes to people all the time and pump up our loved ones, but do we ever tell ourselves how proud we are that we've done this bold thing?

> It takes a lot of guts to start a business.
> When was the last time you sat with that?

(I'll wait while you write that letter to yourself right now. Just meet me back here when that's done. Find a blank spot in this book and just go for it.)

It's a sacred and special thing to create something in the world through your business and then to receive the confirmation that it's valuable to someone else too. When you get paid for this beautiful idea, service, or product, it matters that you honor it.

If you squirm receiving money, this is a memo from your business that it is ready to be reviewed. But it's worth the squirm. When you are rooted in the results you create for that customer, receiving payment is a blessed exchange. You can see the beautiful partnership. You can feel in a correct relationship with the money they choose to invest.

I teach my clients to have a top ten list of the ways your service or product changes their customers' lives for the better. If you are new and haven't yet had a customer, you will need to imagine the results. This will help you move through the squirm of receiving and help you relish in being paid to do what you love.

When you enjoy being paid to do what you love, you are magnetic to more.

When you enjoy being paid to do what you love, you are magnetic to more.

What are your top ten? (Pro tip: These become your most incredible marketing messages!)

Top ten transformations my customers experience:

_____

_____

_____

_____

_____

_____

_____

_____

_____

_____

_____

_____

_____

_____

_____

_____

_____

_____

Worth the Squirm

Liquid Gold Energy

Your energy is liquid gold. Learning where to pour it is wisdom. One of the best outcomes as you heal alongside growing your business is to truly realize and value your energy. The more you heal and squirm, the more you see where you subconsciously squander your energy. The more we respond from a grounded place instead of reflexively reacting, the more life force we have to work with.

You are the biggest asset in your business. Even if you aren't the day-to-day leader anymore, your vision likely still is the torch that lights the way. Your energy matters.

I think about one of my clients who has a factory. They invested in a bigger machine that could crank out their product much more efficiently. It was a game-changer. If that machine broke down, you could bet fixing it was a top priority.

Yet we can wait years to make *ourselves* a top priority. Seeing yourself as the biggest asset in your business and your energy as liquid gold moves you from doer to leader in the best way.

A doer keeps doing. Hamster-wheel style. You run but don't get anywhere. A leader moves a company from surviving to prospering. They can do it without exhausting themselves in the process when they tend to themselves like they would any other critical business asset.

> A leader moves a company from surviving to prospering.

The more we are willing to heal, the more energy we'll discover for what matters. In the messy middle, a ton of rest is required. This is also why treating your energy as liquid gold is a critical component to building your dreams. I teach my clients a concept called the "Top 20" in my Peaceful Planner process. It helps us narrow down what 20 percent of activities lead to 80 percent of our results. It's inspired by the Pareto Principle.[15]

Your energy is liquid gold. Where do you want to pour it? This is your "Top 20."

> Take some time to find your Top 20. For this free tool, head to www.thejuicygoodlife.com and click on "Books" to download the Top 20 worksheet.

Deeper Connections

Do you know what else gets better as we become truer to ourselves and have fewer shoulds stressing us out? Our important relationships. Peace, ease, and joy with our loved ones? Worth the squirm of healing our stuff.

Our wounds come out sideways when we are in the thick of it. I know my old wounds started tons of fights with my husband. My old wounds created pressures that had me in tears with my kids when they were toddlers because I just wanted to do motherhood "right."

My old hustle-and-grind self would put off lunches, pedicures, and movie nights with my besties because I was too busy with a to-do list.

Oof. These are totally opportunities to weaponize my past. I want to cry for old me. She didn't know. But I am not the same lady. I am the lady on the other side of a whole bunch of squirm.

This latest version of me says yes to joy first. This rested version of me has the capacity to deepen my relationships with my husband, son, daughter, and best friends. She has the capacity to do more healing for herself. She has the capacity to be calm, even when life is hard. She's not one straw away from a broken camel's back all the time.

When our wounds run our business and trickle out to our personal lives, we can't see it. We get consumed by the pressure and just try to pack it all in. We martyr ourselves because we don't realize that sacrificing our well-being takes us further away from the person who can deepen our relationships.

> **Sacrificing our well-being takes us further away from the person who can deepen our relationships.**

I think of my client who used to spend several of her private coaching hours with me processing the hurt and frustration she experienced with her husband. Her wounds had her focused on how he didn't understand her, didn't meet her needs or even basic expectations of kindness. To make it worse, he was always complaining about how her business didn't make enough money. The more she wanted to grow her business, the more it brought up all these painful things in her marriage.

There was no special turning point. It wasn't one thing she did to magically feel better. There was no official made-it-through-the-squirm graduation day for her. It was subtle, but over time, as she honored her own needs and dropped the shoulds from her business and marriage, the painful experiences with her husband stopped coming up in coaching.

She now radically embraces who she really is and builds her business around that. She put kiddo time, rest, being creative, and exercising first on her list. She filled her own cup way more than she'd ever given herself permission to before. She squirmed a bit each time she would take a day off in the middle of the week or choose to do an art project with friends on a weekday afternoon. But it wasn't long before she saw the overwhelming happiness that came from deepening her relationship with herself.

> **Healing yourself is the direct route to the deeper, more fulfilling connection you want to have with others.**

After a while, she wasn't looking to her husband to get marriage right. She was busy being herself. She created harmony in her own cells a bit more every day, and pretty soon, her family life was a lot less stressful too. Her whole household benefited from her healing.

Healing yourself is the direct route to the deeper, more fulfilling connection you want to have with others.

The People
We Meet

As if our businesses haven't helped us enough, they can also put us in positions where we get to meet our earth angels. Whether it's finding a coach who helped save your sanity or going to a healer because you're suffering, and they help you unlock new, life-affirming insight, your business will divinely guide you to the humans who help you heal.

If I hadn't been nervous about going into business, I wouldn't have met a reiki practitioner who became my spiritual mentor and cherished friend. If I hadn't started experiencing burnout in my business, I wouldn't have gotten life coaching from one of my future besties, who would teach me to listen to my own needs and introduce me to joy. If I didn't want to lead others better, I wouldn't have pursued getting Dare to Lead certified and met dear friends there.

Had I not wanted to grow my business, I wouldn't have known business coaching existed. Nor would I have met my incredible coaches who have changed my entire life and helped me through the squirm of making my dreams come true.

> Your business will divinely guide you
> to the humans who help you heal.

Without joining a connection group so I could grow my circle, I wouldn't have met clients who would work with me for years and turn into dear friends. Wouldn't have met women who inspire me all around the globe. Without my membership in a coaching group, I wouldn't have met Wendy, who quickly became a bestie and amazing collaborator in my company. Wouldn't have met my soul sister at a networking event, who has been the family I always needed. Our paths may have never crossed if I didn't have my business and if she didn't have hers. Rachelle is my person, and I have my business to thank for bringing her into my life. She has helped me grow personally and professionally in infinite ways. Just this one gift is enough for me to be forever grateful for my business. And I am.

Who do you have your business to thank for bringing into your life?

Magical, isn't it?

Building Trust

As we continue to see progress with each payoff that our business healing creates, we build confidence. We get to show our brain it's working. The next time we are in the squirm, our brain has some new evidence to help it ease up.

This new cycle of squirming, seeing payoffs, and building confidence turns into a newfound trust in yourself and in your business. Each week inside my Should Free Six Figures business growth group, I get to hear my clients share what's working and the wins they experience.

The best thing this coach can hear is her client realizing that she moved through a challenge with more ease, more awareness of what was really at the root of it, and less time spent suffering in it. This is the payoff of building trust.

Women who used to need hours of coaching to get their courage boosted enough to make a decision are now coming back into our group with some sparkle and a newfound swagger, telling us what they are doing to expand their businesses instead of being in paralyzing fear.

I can still see the victorious smile from my friend and client, who had a dream of hosting a retreat on her property but was wobbly in her trust that she could have what she wanted. She got coached, she made a plan, she sold the spots, and she hosted the loveliest, true-to-her-soul retreat.

I can hardly contain my smile remembering that day. I chose to attend because this retreat was totally up my alley. I was jazzed, and I had the best time. When she rolled up on her red three-wheel ATV, she beamed with joy. You could probably see her glow from space—she was so happy. She worked through the squirm of self-doubt and worry. She took the action, she received the payments, she helped her clients. She celebrated.

She built trust in her business that day.

Allow your dreams to take up more space than your anxiousness by living them bit by bit.

Keep letting your business hold up the mirror to what you need to see. Let it be the reflection that transforms you. Allow your dreams to take up more space than your anxiousness by living them bit by bit.

Each time you build a new brain pathway through squirming, celebrating payoffs, and seeing your confidence in action, you build trust. That trust in yourself builds everything you want.

Let's ride, my friends.

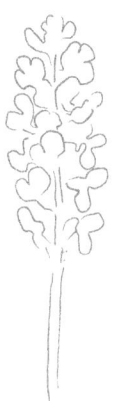

Making Room for Joy

I f you've ever lost someone dear to you, you will know that pain brings a perspective on life that is more potent than most. Think of that person now.

It's okay to cry.

(Hugs, my friend.)

For me, it's my brother, Tanner.

His untimely death kicked down the door to my new life. I asked myself, "What am I waiting for?" when he died.

He lived more life in twenty-seven years than most of us could in one hundred. He wasn't waiting. And I'm not either anymore. It's been a constant evolution since that day in 2009, but I think he'd be really proud of his big sis today.

If you could have another five minutes with them, what do you think they would say to you? What would be their wisdom? I can take a guess. It would have something to do with actually LIVING. Not putting joy off until later. Not taking it all so seriously. They would probably tell you to run toward your dreams. Do the things that matter with the people you love.

Laugh loudly.

Live unapologetically.

Have the adventures.

Our business can be the catalyst for all of it. Can you decide today that you are willing to make room for more joy? To let your business come alongside you and help you build your dreams? Can you choose to love yourself through it?

I do not believe one single ascended soul would come back and tell us to beat ourselves up over something in QuickBooks. Not one single ascended soul would tell us we should take that troll's comment seriously. Not one single ascended soul would tell us that we aren't enough until we hit that next level of revenue.

They wouldn't waste their minutes on misery.

Yet, we continue to fall into this very human trap. Taking it all for granted, day in and day out, until we get that painful perspective. I'm here to invite you to a proactive perspective.

> Run wildly toward joy! Live a life
> that's aligned with your soul!

I'll use all of my liquid gold energy shouting it from the rooftops. My love! Run wildly toward joy! Live a life that's aligned with your soul!

Here's the fun secret: we are more magnetic to the profits we want to create, the impact we want to have, and to the people we want to do life with when we allow ourselves to experience more things that make us feel alive. It took many earth angels along my business healing path to help me get to this point.

I hope this book can be your call up to joy. Whatever joy looks like to you. With every new awareness, with every new moment you choose to love yourself through the squirm of healing, you make room for more joy.

> With every new awareness, with every new moment you choose to love yourself through the squirm of healing, you make room for more joy.

What would help you come alive?

How can you start that right now?

Decide it gets to be juicy good.

Come alive today.
Decide it gets to be juicy good.
I love you.

Thank you,

Sarah

Working Through the Squirm

Ten Steps of the Squirm

Working through the squirm as you grow and heal is a process, my friend. Throughout this book, you likely found spots that resonate, but brains love to know the "how." You might have even skipped to this page before you read the book. It's all good.

Let me break it down to the most basic pieces of how we work through the squirm:

1. Decide.
2. Be rooted in the results you create.
3. Take the next step.
4. Squirm.
5. Add compassion.
6. Decondition with support.
7. Find evidence it's working.
8. Celebrate.
9. Enjoy.
10. Repeat.

1. DECIDE

What empowered decision are you being called upon to make? What dream is calling on your heart? Get clear on what you're deciding. (Bonus for building in boundaries! Example: I am going to write a book, and I am not available for outside naysayers).

2. BE ROOTED IN THE RESULTS YOU CREATE

After we've decided we're going to grow in a new or expanded way, it's most helpful if we set our minds up for success. Remember that Top Ten Transformations list you hopefully made? (In the Getting Paid and Loving It chapter.) Lean on those for this whole process. Come back to your *why*. Come back to your mission and vision.

Write them on sticky notes all over your computer. Read any kind emails or cards or testimonials you've ever received. Strengthen and deepen those roots of truth.

3. TAKE THE NEXT STEP

This can be as simple as taking the tiniest nibble of your plan. It builds momentum. Whatever a next step is, choose it and go. I have really enjoyed making my own blackout bingo cards (thanks for the idea, Wendy!) for my squirmy projects (like this book). It makes it way easier for my old perfectionist tendencies if my steps aren't in a list.

4. SQUIRM

This step may come at any and all points in the process. It doesn't last forever, so let's invite it in. Welcome the squirm as if it were your favorite niece coming home from college for Thanksgiving. Tell her how glad you are to see her and that you want her to sit by you and tell you all the great gossip. You might cringe at some of her stories, but you know she's growing up, and you gotta let her.

Let the squirm sit by you, and befriend it. Accept it with auntie-level warmth.

5. ADD COMPASSION

At some point, the squirm may be bigger than mere discomfort. It might be coming in hot as a trauma response. There is no true solution except loving, compassionate, gentle support. Let it have its say. Suppressing it and bypassing the emotions that want to be felt is not helpful.

Talk to your therapist, your bestie, and your coach. Be witnessed. Go softly through the nervous system activations.

6. DECONDITION

You might be the first person in your circle to be willing to evolve and heal. You might feel as if you are being a rebel or speaking a different language. Your loved ones may project their fears about change and growth onto you. You may have tons of tests and "right on time" moments in this phase. Review your reasons why you want to evolve.

Remind yourself what you're aiming for and why it's worth it to release old limiting beliefs or cultural conditioning and norms. Check in with the people who get it. If you don't have people who get it, I have a community that does, and you are so invited.

7. FIND EVIDENCE IT'S WORKING

Your brain may be in full back-out mode. It will want to take the well-worn path instead of the new growth path every time. Just as an athlete puts good food into their body if they want to perform well, we have to feed our brains the best evidence if we want them to get on board. We have an onboard negativity bias (brains focus way more on the negative) already at work, so don't sleep on any progress.

Stop and give each piece of affirmation a moment of acknowledgment. You can say out loud or write down that it's working! Nothing is too small to notice and name it. (Example: I am marking my bingo card and checking off a list each time I write a new chapter. I'm also making sure to acknowledge every time I come back to the computer after being distracted. It's evidence for my brain that I am capable.)

8. CELEBRATE

Throw all that evidence a little party! Each time we have a small win, celebrate it! I cannot tell you how much of a game-changer this is. Find a few ways you can celebrate, and do it more often than you brush your teeth! We miss the magic in this because we've been conditioned to be "humble." We are here to be alive and expanding our vessel!

Finding a safe space where you can have fun with this is key. My Should Free Six Figures ladies are encouraged to celebrate each dollar they make by taking photos and screenshots of new money coming in, and it is one of the best things we do. What we appreciate, appreciates! What we focus on grows.

It's free to celebrate, it's magnetic as heck, it tells the universe what you'd like to see more of, and it is mission-critical to this entire process.

9. ENJOY

Smell the roses of your growth. This is different than celebrating. This is more along the lines of basking. There is already a payoff (or three) you have created. How can you enjoy it more? Did you take Fridays off finally? Yay! Are you at home, kinda freaking out that you'll be behind on Monday? Nooooo. Enjoy it. Bask. You did the thing; now be present for the payoff!

Perfection is not required. Awareness will make this more lovely.

10. REPEAT

Yep, this is the name of the game. Brains love novelty (hey dopamine, heyyy). At some point, your brain will convince you that you need something new. A new formula, tactic, or even business (hee hee). My friend and past client, Stacy, said something so true once that I think a tattoo of it would be helpful. She said, "It worked so good I stopped doing it!"

Whether it's going to yoga or going through these squirm steps, start again—no shame or shade necessary. Just start again. Bonus points for not being mean to yourself when you forget, get off track, or just want to bail out during the squirm. You are healing, one squirm at a time.

Endnotes

1. Nicole Lewis-Keeber, *How to Love Your Business: Stop Recreating Trauma and Have a Business You Love—and That Loves You Back* (Nicole Lewis-Keeber Coaching, 2021), 46.

2. Simon Sinek, *Start with Why: How Great Leaders Inspire Everyone to Take Action* (New York: Penguin, 2011).

3. Human Design System, https://www.jovianarchive.com.

4. Annie Wright LMFT, "How Parts Work Helps Us Get to Know Ourselves," *Psychology Today*, February 23, 2022, https://www.psychologytoday.com/us/blog/making-the-whole-beautiful/202202/how-parts-work-helps-us-get-to-know-ourselves.

5. Bryan E. Robinson, "The 90-Second Rule That Builds Self-control," *Psychology Today*, April 26, 2020, https://www.psychologytoday.com/ca/blog/the-right-mindset/202004/the-90-second-rule-builds-self-control.

6. Brené Brown, "Brené Brown on How to Reckon with Emotion and Change Your Narrative," *O Magazine*, accessed January 31, 2025, https://www.oprah.com/omagazine/brene-brown-rising-strong-excerpt.

7. Gay Hendricks, T*he Big Leap: A Guide to Transcending Personal Limits, Overcoming Fears, and Unleashing Your Authentic Greatness for a Better Life* (New York: HarperCollins Publishers, 2009), 52.

8. Inspired by Lesson 137, *A Course in Miracles*, https://acim.org/acim/lesson-137/when-i-am-healed-i-am-not-healed-alone/en/s/542.

9. Sherry Gaba LCSW, "The Mother Wound," *Psychology Today*, October 25, 2019, https://www.psychologytoday.com/us/blog/addiction-and-recovery/201910/the-mother-wound.

10. Suzanne Culberg, www.suzanneculberg.com.

11. Don Miguel Ruiz, *The Four Agreements: A Practical Guide to Personal Freedom* (San Rafael, CA: Amber-Allen Publishing, 1997).

12. T. Harv Eker, *Secrets of the Millionaire Mind* (New York: HarperCollins, 2005), 86–88.

13. Melissa Houston, "Breaking The 1.9%: How Women-Owned Businesses Reach $1 Million," *Forbes*, October 10, 2024, https://www.forbes.com/sites/melissahouston/2024/10/10/breaking-the-19-how-women-owned-businesses-reach-1-million/.

14. Hendricks, *The Big Leap*, 1.

15. Marler and Arora, 2004, as cited in "Pareto Principle," ScienceDirect, accessed February 18, 2025, https://www.sciencedirect.com/topics/engineering/pareto-principle.

Recommended Follows

Katie Rubin – katierubin.com

Dr. Jodi Ritsch – joyfuldoc.com

Dr. Aveen Banich – The Wholehearted Healer Podcast

Rachelle Guse – The Eclectic Spark LLC on Facebook

Serena Hicks – serenahicks.com

Nicole Lewis-Keeber – nicole.lewis-keeber.com

Suzanne Culberg – suzanneculberg.com

Wendy Sloneker – goodreads.com/wendysloneker

This Is Not Goodbye

Hi friend,

    Thanks for reading this.
    Thanks for being who you are in the world.
    Thanks for having the courage to build a business.
    It matters. You matter.
    I'm cheering for you.
    I love you.

Sarah

P.S. If you would like to get support with the squirm, that is my specialty.

    My signature program is called Should Free Six Figures, and it enrolls every day of the year.

    Check it out and enroll here:

www.shouldfreesixfigures.com

You are invited to come in to experience the trifecta of incredible business coaching with me, custom business-building training, and the world's most loving, nonjudgmental accountability community.

That's also where you'll find the bonus Peaceful Planner process mentioned in the Workaholism chapter.

If you are curious about my events or working with me privately, you can find those offerings at:

www.thejuicygoodlife.com

Please be sure to hop into my email community when you visit my website. It's where I share more personal insights on business and the squirm of growth.

Let's Stay Connected

I'd love to stay connected and cheer you on.

Find me on social media:

    Facebook: facebook.com/thejuicygoodlife

    LinkedIn: linkedin.com/company/the-juicy-good-life

    Instagram: @juicygoodlife or instagram.com/juicygoodlife

    YouTube: www.youtube.com/@thejuicygoodlife5065

    Threads: threads.net/@juicygoodlife

    Bluesky: @thejuicygoodlife.bsky.social

About the Author

SARAH STOKES is a business breakthrough coach for the open-hearted, overwhelmed over-giver. She helps women "de-should" their businesses to make room for more profits and joy. Her company, The Juicy Good Life, has helped thousands of women create more sustainable and successful businesses through coaching, retreats, and masterminds.

She is an award-winning business strategist who has successfully scaled three companies to multiple millions. Sarah is certified in the leadership work of Dr. Brené Brown and mastermind certified with Tony Robbins. She approaches business growth and sales by being rooted in the true value of the service she provides and loves to help other women do the same.

In her first career, Sarah was a TV news anchor for nearly two decades. She married her co-anchor, Chris, and they exited the TV news world in 2013 to be with their two kids in the evenings instead of at the anchor desk. Sarah's business background includes publishing, scaling, and successfully selling a women's magazine and creating an award-winning global marketing agency that she led for eight years before retiring it so she could be a full-time business coach. Her heart is in philanthropy, and she is happiest hanging out in her pj's on the dock at her lake home or cheering on her kiddos from the sidelines of their multiple sports.

www.ingramcontent.com/pod-product-compliance
Lightning Source LLC
Chambersburg PA
CBHW031433160426
43195CB00010BB/720